British Horror Film Locations

British Horror Film Locations

Derek Pykett

Forewords by
Freddie Francis and Pete Walker

Afterword by Simon Flynn

McFarland & Company, Inc., Publishers
Jefferson, North Carolina, and London

LIBRARY OF CONGRESS CATALOGUING-IN-PUBLICATION DATA

Pykett, Derek.
　　British horror film locations / Derek Pykett ; forewords by Freddie Francis and Pete Walker ; afterword by Simon Flynn.
　　　　p.　　cm.
　　Includes bibliographical references and index.

　　ISBN 978-0-7864-3329-2
　　softcover : 50# alkaline paper ∞

　　1. Horror films — Great Britain — History and criticism   2. Motion picture locations — Great Britain — Guidebooks.   I. Title.
PN1995.9.H6P95   2008
791.43'61640941— dc22   2008019595

British Library cataloguing data are available

©2008 Derek Pykett. All rights reserved

No part of this book may be reproduced or transmitted in any form or by any means, electronic or mechanical, including photocopying or recording, or by any information storage and retrieval system, without permission in writing from the publisher.

On the cover: Sky background ©2007 Shutterstock; *focal* Hermit's Chapel, Roche Rock, Roche, Cornwall; *insets from left* Fountains Abbey, Ripon, North Yorkshire; St. Michael's Mount, Marazion, Cornwall (photos by author); New Lodge, Drift Road, Winkfield, Windsor, Berkshire; Wykehurst Place, Bolney, West Sussex; Black Park, Black Park Road, Wexham, Buckinghamshire (photos by Simon Flynn)

Manufactured in the United States of America

McFarland & Company, Inc., Publishers
　Box 611, Jefferson, North Carolina 28640
　　www.mcfarlandpub.com

This book is in loving memory of my mother,
whom I miss more and more with each passing day;
dedicated to my late friend,
Freddie Francis (1917–2007),
a first-class gentleman, cinematographer,
and unique horror film director;
and for Ruth Potter, the love of my life.

Acknowledgments

Many people have contributed to the production of this book by providing me with help, support, suggestions and invaluable information. They have made this long-overdue reference book possible. They are:

My Dad and my whole family, to whom I shall always be eternally grateful. Without their continuous support, nothing I have done would have been possible.

Luke Pykett, my younger brother, for helping me with my research throughout the writing of this book.

Ruth Potter, my beautiful fiancée, for helping me to hunt out locations in Hertfordshire, and for taking numerous photographs.

Pete Walker and the late Freddie Francis, for taking time out and being kind enough to write the forewords.

Simon Flynn, for writing additional material for this book, and supplying me with over 50 percent of the photographs. To him I am indebted, and enormously grateful.

Colin Beardmore, for finding me addresses and phone numbers of important film personnel, many of whom have helped me during my research. To him I send my deepest thanks.

Terry Pearce, who came forward with some amazing location material, which has enhanced this book 100 percent.

Cecelia Doidge-Ripper, a special friend who, with late husband Michael Ripper, inspired me to write more filmic material.

Brian Holland, a very dear friend, and his wonderful family, who always supply me with endless kindness, support, help and encouragement.

Andrew Thirlwall Potts, my thespian colleague and friend, who is always at hand to help me with research.

Pamela Francis, for helping me to track down some of the locations within this book's pages.

viii Acknowledgments

Sally-Anne Ryan, a special and dear friend who has helped me on several occasions during my research—and never fails to make me laugh.

Sandy Collis and Nick Wright, close friends who are always there when I need someone, both in a private and professional way.

Theresa Doyle, Michael and Karmellah Howlett, Danny R. Fulce, Ian Tyler, Martin Killeen and Elmar Podlasly—who have always been true friends to me, and have made my life a brighter place for it.

Peter Sasdy, Geoffrey Bayldon, Christopher Lee, Sue Atkinson, Norman J. Warren, Kristi Blicharski, Susan Van Den Broek, Richard Fleischer, David Wickes, Melvin Sullivan, Piers Haggard, Jim Clark, Paola Bonelli, Mimsy Farmer, Quentin Falk, Gloria Barclay, Sharon Henson, Darren Perry, Richard Norton, Isobel Blackley, Joe Miller, Denis Ali, Frances Russell, John Harris, Paul Annett, Ronnie Maasz, Keith Topping, Norman Eshley, Bernard Ford, John Hough, Lord Attenborough, Jimmy Sangster, David McGillivray, Peter Jessop, Peter Sinclair, Peter Duffell, Linda Hayden, Val Guest, Tony Reeves, Jean B. Pateman (Highgate Cemetery), Paul Follows (Grim's Dyke Hotel), Jon Beecroft (Oakley Court Hotel), Lee Montague, Neil Binney, Kevin Francis, Sharon Astley (Brocket Hall), Ingo Wiangke (Ettington Park Hotel), Gordon Kingsley (Harlaxton Manor), Roy Ward Baker, Tony Spratling, Iain Wakeford, Jim O'Sullivan (Orford Castle), Andy Jones, Donald Fearney, James Keeble, Beryl Earl, Alan Birkinshaw, Vic Smith, Lord Aldenham, Michael Grant, Dennis Payne, Ann Runeckles, Anthony Waye, Wayne Kinsey, Bushey Library (Hertfordshire), Wilton's Music Hall (London), Matthew Bryant, Simon Sprackling, Ken Baker, Nick Daubeny, Malcolm Middleton, Brian Daubney, Diane Halfpenny (National Trust/Ashridge Estate), Robert Bard—to all of the above, a big thank you, and I shall always be forever grateful.

Illustrations Courtesy of: Simon Flynn, Ruth Potter, Terry Pearce, Sally-Anne Ryan, Freddie Francis, Ettington Park Hotel, Elmar Podlasly, Orford Castle, Wayne Kinsey, Wykehurst Place, Alan Hughes, Brian Holland and Kate Holland.

Table of Contents

Acknowledgments	vii
Forewords by Freddie Francis and Pete Walker	1
Introduction	5
On Location: The Masters of Horror	9
The Films (with Locations)	11
The Studios	135
Locations — In Detail	147
What Was Filmed Where?	187
Hammer House of Horror	191
Afterword: Location Hunting by Simon Flynn	195
Bibliography	197
Index	199

Foreword
by Freddie Francis

Very rarely on any of the horror movies I directed did we have the budget to film on location. When we did get the chance, I always enjoyed it much more than being confined within a studio space. Also, being a cinematographer, it is much more interesting to the eye to film at a real location.

So, having used a few of the locations revealed in this book, I am delighted that Derek Pykett has researched and listed them so well.

I have no doubt they will be of interest to many fans who will be able to identify them (or not!), together with the many grisly events that might, or might not, have taken place there.

Isleworth, London

Films listed: *Craze* (1974), *The Creeping Flesh* (1972), *Dr. Terror's House of Horrors* (1965), *Dracula Has Risen from the Grave* (1968), *The Elephant Man* (1980), *The Ghoul* (1974), *The Innocents* (1961), *Legend of the Werewolf* (1974), *Son of Dracula* (1974), *Tales from the Crypt* (1972), *Trog* (1970)

Foreword
by Pete Walker

When I first started taking an interest in movies, probably at eleven or twelve years of age, one of the first things I learned was the enormous cost of film making which has always been hard to come to terms with. Even in the

Freddie Francis (center) directing one of his many horror movies. Courtesy of Freddie Francis.

1930s, for example, the Astaire-Rogers films apparently nearly broke RKO Radio Pictures mainly because of the cost of the sets. It is said that the black marble ballroom set for *The Gay Divorcee* cost one million dollars in 1934, the era of deco super–dance halls which existed in many towns in the USA.

"Why could they not have made it on location?" I said to my production manager when he showed me around the studio ballroom set of the film he was working on, *The Ruling Class*, in 1972. "We're paying £6,000 a day for the hire of that chandelier," he said, pointing to an enormous glass contraption hoisted up into the gantry. "It's been there for three weeks already and we haven't started shooting on this set yet." Every production crew will have stories of mind-boggling waste and excesses of course. Even as a teenage bit player in black-and-white "B" movies around the early '60s, I was amazed that these Poverty Row movies would be constructing ordinary living rooms or kitchens — sparsely furnished and with very little atmosphere — in studios, when the entire film could well have been shot on location, with the money saved spent on a better cast to enhance the salability of the product.

It's not only because of costs, of course, that films are made on location, so it's time that a book devoted to movie locations — particularly horror movies — hits the book stands. I am delighted that Derek Pykett has asked me to say a few words as one of those "cheapskate" producers-directors who never gave his cast and crew the "comfort" of a studio-based picture. I'm kidding, of course. I really do think that real locations add so much more atmosphere and authenticity to a picture. Not always possible with period horror films but certainly with the modern dress "terror" films that I made.

Finally, an amusing parable. I remember desperately trying to find a disused prison for *House of Whipcord*. After weeks of fruitless search and pestering virtually every chief constable throughout the UK (I even spent a week in

Northern and Southern Ireland), I set to work on the Home Office and inundated them for days on end with phone calls, refusing to take "no" for an answer. It was the time of the Heath government in the UK and I eventually got a call from an irate home secretary! "You've been driving my department mad, Mr. Walker!" he screamed at me. "Now what the hell is it that we can do for you?" I told him what I was looking for. "Disused prison?" he spluttered, "Now I know you're mad. I'm looking for a few of those myself— if you find one let me know and I'll re-open it!" and he slammed down the phone.

Enjoy *British Horror Film Locations*. It's a novel and interesting piece and I am sure will be enjoyed by all lovers of horror movies and those fascinated by the making of them.

Esher, Surrey

Films listed: *The Comeback* (1977), *The Flesh and Blood Show* (1972), *Frightmare* (1974), *House of the Long Shadows* (1982), *House of Mortal Sin* (1975), *House of Whipcord* (1974)

Introduction

Did you ever wonder, many years ago, when you hid beneath a cushion and watched those late night horror films, where certain scenes were filmed? If those gothic mansions and creepy-looking graveyards were actually real places, and not just some set on a back lot at a studio? I did, often, but I never came across any.

It was only by chance that in 2002 I stumbled across Camelot Castle in Tintagel, Cornwall, while visiting a dear friend, Brian Holland. This impressive-looking hotel, standing on a cliff's edge, was used in the 1979 *Dracula* film with Frank Langella and Laurence Olivier — and it was here that my location hunting would begin. Not just any old locations, but classic (and sometimes not so classic) British horror film locations, my intention being to include as many horror movies and their locations as humanly possible, starting with the first ever British sound chiller, *Castle Sinister,* made way back in 1932; the classic horrors of the '50s, '60s and '70s, made mainly by Hammer and Amicus; and including more recent fright fests like *The Hole* and the smash hit horror comedy *Shaun of the Dead.* Not all are British; you'll find here Italy's *The Living Dead at the Manchester Morgue* and America's *Interview with the Vampire.* Some are even international made-for-television horrors, like the lavish David Wickes productions *Jack the Ripper* and *Jekyll & Hyde.* But all have one thing in common: they were shot almost entirely within the British Isles, and this is why I include them.

Originally, I thought this book would be an easy task, and I would have it completed after a year. Five years later, I'm finally putting the coffin lid on it, and it's proved to be one of the biggest challenges of my life. Why? Because information of this kind is limited, almost unavailable anywhere. The British Film Institute in London holds nothing in its archives, as I discovered with actor-friend Andrew Thirlwall Potts, and I almost cried upon discovering so. What I regard as a quite important reference, hadn't even been logged into their computers. So I shall be making sure that a copy of this book goes to them, as no British Film Institute should be without such.

6 Introduction

How did I do it? Well, first of all I had to be 100 percent dedicated to the project, and be prepared to put in many hours of research. But it would never have been possible without the many people, including numerous important film personnel, who have gone out of their way to help me locate those creepy (and sometimes not so creepy) locations which added to the atmosphere of those chillers.

Some locations eluded me for the full five years, like Thorpe House in Surrey, which appears in *The Creeping Flesh*, while others were easy to find. But I really had nothing to go on, other than the word of someone who may have worked on the films concerned.

It's therefore been a struggle, and at one point I was actually going to abandon the whole project, as it was proving too difficult, and beginning to give me real nightmares. In fact, I wouldn't have carried on if it wasn't for my dear friends Pamela and the late Freddie Francis, who gave me a word of encouragement; I knew I must battle on. It was worth it, and I've managed to find out more than I ever dreamed possible. I never would have thought that I would get past 80 films, but I did.

Simon Flynn must not have realized what he was letting himself in for when I asked him to photograph a few places, which turned out to be several dozen, with him having to go back to a place more than once in order for us to correctly identify it. Which, of course, is the hardest part, matching up your photographs with what you see on the screen. Not an easy task, and I would send poor Simon back to places several times until I was satisfied with what I saw. I am convinced that every location featured in this book is the very same location you see in the film. Most were actually confirmed as the right place by film personnel, others we identified ourselves after careful research.

The tomb of Mary Wollstonecraft Shelley: St. Peter's Church, Hinton Road, Bournemouth. (Photograph by the author.)

Many of the places though are unmistakable, even on first sight, and it has been very exciting to see some of them up close, as several are quite historic. It is important to note that many of the locations featured are private residences, and I would therefore be grateful if the privacy of the individuals who live there is respected.

I hope this book will

entertain you as much as it has entertained me to write it and compile the photographs. It includes information which has never been put in print before. It has taken myself, Simon Flynn, my fiancée Ruth Potter, the incredibly kind-hearted Terry Pearce (who took time out of a very busy TV schedule to help me out) as well as numerous other individuals on many mystery tours. We sometimes stumbled into things we were not expecting, like the tomb of Mary Wollstonecraft Shelley, and the London home of Bram Stoker. It's been fun, and sometimes a little bit annoying, when things were not quite going as planned. But we've made it, all in one piece.

The most exciting part for me was when Terry Pearce, who worked as an assistant director on several classic horror movies, including *Tales from the Crypt* and *Frankenstein: The True Story* furnished me with his shooting scripts, which of course listed all the locations. This material is very rarely kept by film personnel, and so when someone like Terry comes forward with it you know you have something special.

The London home of Bram Stoker: 18 St. Leonard's Terrace, Chelsea. (Photograph by the author.)

This book may never have been completed without the invaluable written contributions of Simon Flynn, Sally-Anne Ryan and Brian Holland. Their segments throughout this book have certainly enlightened its pages and brought to my work other people's perspectives on some of the locations concerned.

My only hope now is that it will be of interest to people who love the British horror film, as I have certainly given away lots of little secrets which could have been lost forever if I hadn't pushed ahead with the project five years ago.

These five years have been the most difficult of my life, not because of the book, but because I lost the one person who encouraged and supported me in everything I did — my mother. She was thrilled when I started this project, but, sad to say, is not here to see the finished product. This book is therefore in memory of my mum, because if she hadn't introduced me to horror films at the tender age of six, this would probably have never been written. To my mum I am eternally grateful: I hope that she is shining down on me, and is able to see the book's completion.

Derek Pykett
Unstone, Derbyshire

On Location: The Masters of Horror

All the great horror stars have filmed on location in the UK.

My favorite amongst these shall always be the gentleman that was Peter Cushing, as his kindness to me over an eight-year period is something I shall never forget. Even in ill health, during the last years of his life, he was still as polite and courteous as ever, living quietly by the sea in Whistable, Kent. He was most certainly one of a kind, and I, for one, shall forever miss his loving personality and wonderful sense of humor.

As regards Peter Cushing locations, the one to look out for is Rotherfield House in Hampshire, where Peter, Christopher Lee, Vincent Price and even John Carradine filmed *House of the Long Shadows*. The movie was shot nearly entirely on location, both exterior and interior.

Grim's Dyke Hotel in Harrow Weald, just outside London, played host to Peter when he shot *Blood Beast Terror* on its grounds. But it has also seen Boris Karloff and Christopher Lee there for *The Curse of the Crimson Altar*. Vincent Price shot on location at Grim's Dyke for *Cry of the Banshee*, and the legendary horror writer, Bram Stoker, was a guest there on many occasions during the early part of the twentieth century.

A location that turns up in more horror films than any other is Windsor's Oakley Court, now a hotel. Both Peter Cushing and Lon Chaney, Jr., have appeared on film at its grand entrance: Peter in *The Brides of Dracula* and Chaney in *Witchcraft*.

The only other great master of the horror film is Bela Lugosi, and he filmed in the UK on three occasions. The first time was in 1935 when he appeared in *The Mystery of the Mary Celeste* for Hammer Films. The last was when he appeared in the horror-comedy *Mother Riley Meets the Vampire*. Unfortunately, most of his scenes in these films were studio-bound, both filmed at the same studio, Nettlefold Studios in Walton-on-Thames, Surrey, which had most of its sound stages and buildings demolished in the 1960s. However, one part of the studio does still exist on its original site — Hurst Grove. (See the chapter "The Studios" for a more in-depth look.)

It is nice to know that all the great Masters of Horror filmed on British soil, and that the places above shall forever hold those memories.

The Films (with Locations)

The Abominable Dr. Phibes
American International Pictures (1971)

Cast: Vincent Price, Joseph Cotten, Hugh Griffith, Terry-Thomas, Peter Jeffrey, Virginia North, Aubrey Woods, Peter Gilmore, John Cater, Caroline Munro.
Screenplay: James Whiton, William Goldstein.
Producers: Louis M. Heyward, Ron Dunas.
Director: Robert Fuest.

A man who was horribly disfigured in the car accident that also took the life of his wife, seeks revenge on those whom he considers responsible.

Studio: Elstree Studios, Borehamwood, Hertfordshire.
Location: Phibes Mansion (exterior): Caldecote Towers, Elstree Road, Bushey Heath, Bushey, Hertfordshire, WD23.

The striking-looking and unmissable nineteenth-century building as seen from Elstree Road, Caldecote Towers, was the ideal setting for the home of Dr. Phibes (Vincent Price) and his corpse bride, Victoria (Caroline Munro).

Caldecote was built in 1832 as a private house by a Captain Marjoribanks Loftus Otway. In 1891, it became Caldecote Towers School, and then in 1926 Rosary Priory, a convent and boarding school, when it was bought by the Dominican Sisters of St. Catherine of Siena. They sold it in 1988, and it is now Immanuel College, a Jewish secondary school.

Caldecote also featured in episodes of the cult British television series *The Avengers*, including the episode "The Master Minds."

An American Werewolf in London
Lycanthrope Films (1981)

Cast: David Naughton, Griffin Dunne, Jenny Agutter, Brian Glover, John Woodvine, David Schofield, Rik Mayall, Frank Oz, Paul Kember, Sydney Bromley, Michael Carter.
Producers: Peter Guber, Jon Peters.
Screenplay-Director: John Landis.

Two young American male backpackers are attacked by a werewolf while out walking on the Yorkshire moors.

Studio: Twickenham Film Studios, Middlesex.
Locations: Village of East Proctor (including exterior of The Slaughtered Lamb): Crickadarn, Powys, Wales.

The Slaughtered Lamb (interior): The Black Swan, Old Lane, Martyr's Green, Cobham, Surrey, KT11 1NG.

Nurse Price's Flat (exterior and interior): 64 Coleherne Road, Kensington, London, SW10.

London Underground: Tottenham Court Road.

Piccadilly Circus: Piccadilly Circus, London, W1.

End Alleyway: Winchester Walk, Southwark, London, SE1.

The tiny Welsh village of Crickadarn doubles as the Yorkshire village of East Proctor, where David Naughton and Griffin Dunne stumble across the pub The Slaughtered Lamb, which is actually a private house. The interiors of the pub were filmed at The Black Swan in Surrey, which has recently been refurbished.

Jenny Agutter's flat (64 Coleherne Road, Kensington), where David Naughton first be-

The Abominable Dr. Phibes: Doubling as the home of Dr. Phibes (Vincent Price) is Caldecote Towers, Elstree Road, Bushey, Hertfordshire. Courtesy of Ruth Potter.

An American Werewolf in London: Crickadarn, Powys, Wales, doubled as the village of East Proctor (including exterior of "The Slaughtered Lamb"). Courtesy of Sally-Anne Ryan.

comes the werewolf, has remained totally unchanged since 1981. It is part of a private residence.

The scenes featuring the businessman (Michael Carter) being chased through the London Underground by the werewolf, were shot at Tottenham Court Road, and also on the platform.

One of the most famous, and daring, horror movie sequences ever filmed is the Piccadilly Circus sequence with cars and buses swerving and crashing to avoid the snarling lycanthrope, causing complete mayhem in the heart of central London. To achieve this incredible scene, director John Landis had to employ many stuntmen (including himself). Piccadilly Circus itself had to be closed (for the first time ever) for filming on two successive nights, with the more complicated stunt sequences having to be staged on a replica set on the back lot at Twickenham Film Studios.

An American Werewolf in London: 64 Coleherne Road, Kensington, London, featured as the flat of Nurse Price (Jenny Agutter). (Photograph by the author.)

The end sequence, in which the werewolf (Naughton) is cornered and shot in an alleyway, was filmed on Winchester Walk in Southwark, London.

And Now the Screaming Starts!
Amicus Films (1972)

Cast: Peter Cushing, Herbert Lom, Stephanie Beacham, Patrick Magee, Ian Ogilvy, Geoffrey Whitehead, Guy Rolfe, Rosalie Crutchley, Janet Key, Gillian Lind, Lloyd Lamble, Norman Mitchell.
Screenplay: Roger Marshall.
Producers: Max J. Rosenberg, Milton Subotsky.
Director: Roy Ward Baker.

A newlywed discovers that she is living in a country house that has been under a curse for many years.

An American Werewolf in London: The werewolf (David Naughton) is cornered and shot on Winchester Walk, Southwark, London. (Photograph by the author.)

Studio: Shepperton Studios, Middlesex.
Location: House of Fengriffen (exterior): Oakley Court Hotel, Windsor Road, Water Oakley, Windsor, SL4 5UR.

See the chapter "Locations — In Detail" for an in-depth look at Oakley Court, which doubles as the haunted house of newlywed Charles Fengriffen (Ian Ogilvy) and bride Catherine (Stephanie Beacham).

Used in more horror movies than any other place, Oakley Court is at its most spooky in *Vampyres*, and at its most beautiful in *And Now The Screaming Starts!* It is now a high-class luxury hotel, set in very beautiful grounds, nesting beside the river Thames.

In daylight the place is stunning, but it could possibly be a bit spooky at night. How-

***And Now the Screaming Starts!*:** The home of newlywed Charles Fengriffen (Ian Ogilvy) and bride Catherine (Stephanie Beacham) is Oakley Court Hotel, Water Oakley, Windsor. Courtesy of Simon Flynn.*

ever, next to Wykehurst Place (Hell House in *The Legend of Hell House*), it looks more like a child's playhouse.

The Anniversary
Hammer Films (1968)

Cast: Bette Davis, Jack Hedley, James Cossins, Sheila Hancock, Elaine Taylor, Timothy Bateson.
Screenplay-Producer: Jimmy Sangster.
Director: Roy Ward Baker.

A malevolent one-eyed widow will stop at nothing to prevent her grown sons from leaving the family orbit.

*"The most terrifying thing about Oakley isn't its horror past, with Dracula, Frankenstein's Monster and vampires running amok in its grounds. No, this is nowhere near as terrifying as receiving your bill after a cup of tea and a scone"—Simon Flynn.

The Anniversary: "Chantry," Barnet Lane, Elstree, Borehamwood, Hertfordshire, doubles as the home of Mrs. Taggart (Bette Davis). Courtesy of Simon Flynn.*

Studio: Elstree Studios, Borehamwood, Hertfordshire.
Location: Mrs. Taggart's House (exterior): Chantry, Barnet Lane, Elstree, Borehamwood, Hertfordshire, WD6 3RA.

The Chantry in Elstree, a beautiful, large, modern-looking house, played home to Mrs. Taggart (Bette Davis). It is just a few minutes' walk from the Edgwarebury Corus Hotel, which is also along Barnet Lane, where Hammer filmed *The Devil Rides Out*.

As a note of interest, the Chantry was at one time used on a rental basis by Elstree Film Studios to house their transitory stars. Among those that stayed there included Yul Brynner, Elizabeth Taylor, Gregory Peck, Audrey Hepburn, Anthony Quinn, and the former U.S. president, Ronald Reagan. One of the more dramatic events for which this house is remembered was the theft of Sophia Loren's jewelry while she was staying there.

Asylum (1972)
Amicus Films

Cast: Robert Powell, Herbert Lom, Patrick Magee, Geoffrey Bayldon, Bar-

---

*"A very grand house. Definitely worth a few bucks. But nothing sinister or unusual about this one. Just a warm, private, family home"—Simon Flynn.

bara Parkins, Richard Todd, Sylvia Syms, Peter Cushing, Barry Morse, Britt Ekland, Charlotte Rampling, James Villiers, Megs Jenkins.
Screenplay: Robert Bloch.
Producers: Max J. Rosenberg, Milton Subotsky.
Director: Roy Ward Baker.

A doctor, applying for a new job at an asylum, hears weird stories from the inmates, but finds himself in the middle of a weirder one.

Studio: Shepperton Studios, Middlesex.
Locations: Dunsmoor Asylum (exterior): New Lodge, Drift Road, Winkfield, Windsor, Berkshire, SL4 4RQ.
Dunsmoor Asylum (interior): Littleton Park House, Shepperton Studios, Studios Road, Shepperton, Middlesex, TW17 OQD.

See the chapter "Locations — In Detail" for an in-depth look at New Lodge, which doubles here as the exterior to the Dunsmoor Asylum.

If you travel to New Lodge on the road from Maidenhead, Berkshire, you pass it on the right, and as you do so, you will feel like you are Robert Powell in the film. The entrance to the property is gated, guarded by two griffins. It hasn't been altered whatsoever. In fact, you expect to see Geoffrey Bayldon peek through the wooden door saying, "It keeps out the draft, as Dr. Starr used to say."

The interior to Dunsmoor is Littleton Park House at Shepperton Studios, which is also known as Shepperton Old House. The reception hall with its checkered black-and-white marbled floor features several times in the movie, as does the staircase, where Powell looks at the sinister paintings on the wall. The house is surrounded by spectacular grounds. It was built in 1689, and is used today mainly as a reception venue for weddings.

The Asylum
Nunhead Films (2000)

Cast: Steffanie Pitt, Nick Waring, Ingrid Pitt, Patrick Mower, Robin Askwith, Colin Baker, Robin Parkinson.
Producer: Carol Lemon.
Screenplay-Director: John Stewart

A young woman returns to a disused asylum to try and uncover the truth about her mother's murder.

Location: The Asylum (exterior and interior): Old Netherne Hospital, Netherne on the Hill, Coulsdon, Surrey, CR5.
Simon Flynn writes: The town of Coulsdon, not far from Croydon, Surrey, is where I grew up, and believe it or not it had two asylums. One which is

still in operation is the sinister-looking and named Cane Hill, in which both David Bowie and Michael Caine had brothers in residence. But Netherne Hospital, built in 1905, closed about the time the above film was made there. Back then, Netherne was really just an area of housing (in which the hospital staff would once have lived), and several buildings sprawled over both sides of the road. There must have been ten big wards-wings. These became vacant over the years, until the end of the 1990s, and the few remaining patients were kept in an area near the main building. Then, one by one, buildings started to be knocked down, until all that remained of the original asylum was the main entrance, the clock tower, and a nearby church (which is no longer in use). This stands on the grounds, and would have been the hospital chapel. The hospital even had its own burial ground. All these buildings still stand and can be seen in the film. Now though, in 2006, things could not be more different. You can view new homes in the area and the slogan on their billboards is *Netherne on the Hill—A village comes to life.* This is true, as it is indeed now a village, with a post office, many houses and a park, etc. Years ago there was no such place: Netherne on the Hill did not exist, Netherne was just the name of the hospital, which was the only thing in this rural area. It is without doubt an interesting movie location. They actually filmed inside the hospital too, putting the long, grim corridors to good use. Splendid stuff.

The Awakening
EMI Films (1980)

Cast: Charlton Heston, Susannah York, Jill Townsend, Stephanie Zimbalist, Patrick Drury, Bruce Meyers, Ian McDiarmid, Miriam Margolyes, Michael Mellinger, Leonard Maguire
Screenplay: Allan Scott, Chris Bryant, Clive Exton
Producer: Robert Solo
Director: Mike Newell

After 3,800 years, an Egyptian queen is reincarnated in the body of the daughter of the archaeologist who opens her tomb.

Studio: Elstree Studios, Borehamwood, Hertfordshire.
Location: The British Museum (exterior): University College, Gower Street, London, WC1E 6BT.

Founded in 1826, the University College in central London doubles as the British Museum, where Charlton Heston displays a rather deadly Egyptian find.

The Awakening: University College, Gower Street, London, doubles as the British Museum. (Photograph by the author.)

The Beast in the Cellar
Tigon Films (1970)

Cast: Flora Robson, Beryl Reid, John Hamill, T.P. McKenna, Tessa Wyatt, Christopher Chittell, Roberta Tovey
Producers: Tony Tenser, Graham Harris
Screenplay-Director: James Kelly

Two unmarried sisters hide their demented brother in the cellar, but he escapes and goes on a murderous rampage.

Studio: Pinewood Studios, Buckinghamshire.
Location: Railway Station — Victorian Flashback Sequence: Bluebell Railway, Sheffield Park Station, Nr. Uckfield, East Sussex, TN22 2QL.

The Bluebell Railway is the U.K.'s only all-steam railway with a large collection of steam locomotives and authentic period stations dating from Victorian times. It is therefore quite frequently used as a film location, and features here briefly in a flashback sequence.

The Beast in the Cellar: Bluebell Railway, Nr. Uckfield, East Sussex, features briefly in a Victorian flashback sequence. Courtesy of Simon Flynn.

The Beast Must Die
Amicus Films (1973)

Cast: Calvin Lockhart, Peter Cushing, Charles Gray, Anton Diffring, Marlene Clark, Ciaran Madden, Michael Gambon, Tom Chadbon
Screenplay: Michael Winder
Producer: Milton Subotsky
Director: Paul Annett

A millionaire big-game hunter holds a weekend party to track down a werewolf, which is hiding somewhere among his guest list.

Studio: Shepperton Studios, Middlesex.
Location: Newcliffe's Country House (exterior and interior): Littleton Park House, Shepperton Studios, Studios Road, Shepperton, Middlesex, TW17 0QD.

See *Asylum* (1972) for details about Littleton Park House, which doubles here as Tom Newcliffe's country home, where one of his invited guests is a werewolf.

The Black Cat: The tiny village of Hambledon, Nr. Marlow, Buckinghamshire, can be seen during the opening credits and throughout the film. (Photograph by the author.)

The Black Cat
Italian International Film (1981)

Cast: Patrick Magee, Mimsy Farmer, David Warbeck, Al Cliver, Dagmar Lassander, Bruno Corazzari, Geoffrey Copleston, Daniela Dorio
Screenplay: Biagio Proietti, Lucio Fulci
Producer: Giulio Sbarigia
Director: Lucio Fulci

A detective is sent to investigate a series of murders in an English village, but it is a female photographer who connects them to a strange man's sinister cat.

Locations: The Village: Hambleden, Nr. Marlow, Buckinghamshire and West Wycombe Village, High Wycombe, Buckinghamshire.

This cult Italian horror is notable as it was the only time Lucio Fulci would film one of his chillers entirely on location in England, with two places actually doubling as the village. Firstly, the tiny village of Hambleden, which can be seen during the opening credits (with the black cat walking along the school roof, etc.), as well as appearing throughout the film in scenes with David Warbeck and Mimsy Farmer.

The second location is West Wycombe Village; the Main Street with its buildings from the fifteenth to nineteenth century is featured on several occasions.

The Black Torment
Compton Films (1964)

Cast: John Turner, Heather Sears, Ann Lynn, Peter Arne, Francis De Wolff, Raymond Huntley, Patrick Troughton, Norman Bird
Screenplay: Donald Ford, Derek Ford
Producer-Director: Robert Hartford-Davis

A baronet begins to fear for his own sanity following a series of nasty incidents that appear to be his own handiwork.

Studio: Shepperton Studios, Middlesex.
Location: Fordyke Hall (exterior and interior): The Vyne, Sherborne St. John, Basingstoke, RG24 9HL.

The Vyne is an impressive sixteenth century manor house (open to the public), set in beautiful surroundings, dating back to Henry VIII's reign (see the chapter "Locations — In Detail" for a more in-depth look). It doubles here as Fordyke Hall, the family seat of Sir Richard Fordyke (John Turner), a man on the verge of insanity.

Blind Terror
Genesis Productions Limited (1971)

Cast: Mia Farrow, Robin Bailey, Dorothy Alison, Diane Grayson, Norman Eshley, Brian Rawlinson, Christopher Matthews, Paul Nicholas, Michael Elphick, Donald Bissett
Screenplay: Brian Clemens
Producer: Leslie Linder
Director: Richard Fleischer

A blind girl, the sole survivor of a killer's murderous rampage on a lonely country estate, is now hunted by the fiend.

Studio: Shepperton Studios, Middlesex.
Location: Manor Farm (exterior and interior): Binfield Manor, Binfield Road, Binfield, Nr. Bracknell, Berkshire.

Doubling as Manor Farm is Binfield Manor, a large private country house in which Sarah (Mia Farrow) is stalked by insane killer Jacko (Paul Nicholas).

Blood Beast Terror
Tigon Films (1968)

    Cast: Peter Cushing, Robert Flemyng, Wanda Ventham, Vanessa Howard, David Griffin, Glynn Edwards, Roy Hudd
    Screenplay: Peter Bryan
    Producer: Arnold L. Miller
    Director: Vernon Sewell

The daughter of a Victorian entomologist can change herself into a giant, murderous death's head moth.

    Studio: Goldhawk Studios, Shepherd's Bush, London.
    Location: Clare House (exterior): Grim's Dyke Hotel, Old Redding, Harrow Weald, London, HA3 6SH.

See the chapter "Locations—In Detail" for an in-depth look at Grim's Dyke Hotel, which features here as the home of Dr. Mallinger (Robert Flemyng), who is up to some rather bizarre scientific business in his cellar.

Blood on Satan's Claw
Tigon Films (1970)

    Cast: Patrick Wymark, Linda Hayden, Barry Andrews, Simon Williams, Tamara Ustinov, Michele Dotrice, Wendy Padbury, Anthony Ainley, James Hayter, Charlotte Mitchell, Robin Davies, Howard Goorney
    Screenplay: Robert Wynne-Simmons
    Producers: Tony Tenser, Malcolm B. Heyworth, Peter L. Andrews
    Director: Piers Haggard

The discovery of a devil's claw sparks of devil worship amongst a group of farm children in a seventeenth century English village.

    Studio: Pinewood Studios, Buckinghamshire.
    Location: Church Ruins: St. James Church (derelict), Bix, Henley-on-Thames, Oxfordshire.

St. James Church was built in the early 1600s; its ruins can be seen in several scenes throughout the film, including the rape sequence featuring Wendy Padbury. It also features heavily in the climax with Patrick Wymark. St. James itself ceased as a church in 1874, and the consecrated ground and building are today cared for by English Heritage.

This derelict church has a horror story to tell of its own: In 1974, vandals invaded the site and in the early hours of the morning indulged in some black magic rituals, even using bones from the graves they desecrated.

The Brides of Dracula
Hammer Films (1960)

Cast: Peter Cushing, David Peel, Freda Jackson, Martita Hunt, Yvonne Monlaur, Mona Washbourne, Henry Oscar, Miles Malleson
Screenplay: Jimmy Sangster, Peter Bryan, Edward Percy
Producer: Anthony Hinds
Director: Terence Fisher

Baron Meinster, a disciple of Dracula, is locked in a room by his mother. An unsuspecting young woman lets him out and he goes on a rampage.

The Brides of Dracula: The entrance to Oakley Court Hotel, Water Oakley, Windsor, doubles as the grand entrance to Chateau Meinster. Courtesy of Simon Flynn.

Studio: Bray Studios, Windsor, Berkshire.
Location: Chateau Meinster Entrance: Oakley Court Hotel, Windsor Road, Water Oakley, Windsor, SL4 5UR.
Woodland: Black Park, Black Park Road, Wexham, Buckinghamshire, SL3 6DR.

The entrance to Oakley Court with its two griffins can be seen briefly when Peter Cushing, as Van Helsing, chases the evil Baron Meinster (David Peel), through its doorway. The opening of the film, with Michael Ripper speeding through the misty woodland on his coach and horses, was shot in Black Park, a popular parkland set (530 acres of attractive woodland, grassland and heathland with a centerpiece lake — which is also seen in the movie). Black Park was used by Hammer on many occasions, and has also been a location in many other films, including the James Bond and Harry Potter series.

The Brides of Dracula: The Woodland Sequences were filmed at Black Park, Black Park Road, Wexham, Buckinghamshire. Courtesy of Simon Flynn.*

Carry on Screaming
Anglo-Amalgamated Productions (1966)

Cast: Harry H. Corbett, Kenneth Williams, Fenella Fielding, Charles Hawtrey, Jim Dale, Angela Douglas, Peter Butterworth, Bernard Bresslaw, Jon Pertwee, Frank Thornton
Screenplay: Talbot Rothwell
Producer: Peter Rogers
Director: Gerald Thomas

A pair of bungling policemen investigate a mad doctor and his sister who, with the help of a couple of hairy beasts, are turning young women into mannequins.

Studio: Pinewood Studios, Buckinghamshire.

"Black Park is a very big park, and extremely scenic. It is also very calm and peaceful. For some reason though I still expected to see a horse-drawn carriage come rattling past, or maybe even Count D. himself." — Simon Flynn

Location: Bide-A-Wee Rest Home (exterior): Fulmer Grange, Teikyo School U.K., Framewood Road, Wexham, Buckinghamshire, SL2 4QS.

Doubling as the creepy home of, Dr. Watt (Kenneth Williams) is Fulmer Grange, a former Victorian house which now stands as part of a Japanese school.

Castle Sinister
Delta (1932)

Cast: Haddon Mason, Eric Adeney, Wally Patch, Edmund Kennedy
Screenplay-Producer-Director: Widgey R. Newman

A mad scientist conducts unspeakable experiments in his basement laboratory.

Studio: Bushey Film Studios, Melbourne Road, Bushey, Hertfordshire.

This, the first British sound horror film, was made on the cheap as a B picture entirely on sound stages at Bushey Film Studios (see the chapter "The Studios" for a more in-depth look). *Castle Sinister* was a poorly received film, and the British censor was horrified by it, therefore making it sink instantly into obscurity. Today it rarely surfaces, which is a shame as it played quite a large part in the history of the British horror film.

Children of the Damned
Metro-Goldwyn-Mayer (1964)

Cast: Ian Hendry, Alan Badel, Barbara Ferris, Alfred Burke, Sheila Allen, Ralph Michael, Harold Goldblatt, Patrick Wymark
Screenplay: John Briley
Producer: Ben Arbeid
Director: Anton M. Leader

Six super-intelligent children are brought to England from around the world for scientific study. They turn out to be invaders from another planet.

Studio: MGM Studios, Borehamwood, Hertfordshire.
Location: Church Sequences: St. Dunstan-in-the-East, St. Dunstans Hill, London, EC3.

St. Dunstan's Church, now nothing more than a ruin after it was severely damaged in the blitz in 1941, was originally built in 1100. It features in the climax of the movie, with the children taking up residence there.

A Clockwork Orange
Hawk Films (1971)

Cast: Malcolm McDowell, Michael Bates, Adrienne Corri, Patrick Magee, Warren Clarke, Miriam Karlin, Aubrey Morris, John Savident, Anthony Sharp, Philip Stone, Dave Prowse
Producer: Bernard Williams
Screenplay-Director: Stanley Kubrick

In a future Britain of desolation and violence, a young gangster guilty of rape and murder obtains a release from prison after being experimentally brainwashed, only to find society more violent than it was in his time.

Studio: Elstree Studios, Borehamwood, Hertfordshire.
Locations: Subway: Northern Subway, Trinity Road, Wandsworth, London, SW17.
Woodmere Health Farm (exterior): Manor Lodge School, Rectory Lane, Ridge Hill, Shenley, Hertfordshire, WD7 9BG.

The opening of the film, in which the droogs, headed by Malcolm McDowell, senselessly beat up an old tramp, was filmed in the Northern Subway in Wandsworth.

Doubling as the Woodmere Health Farm, where Miriam Karlin is terrorized by the droogs, is Manor Lodge School.

Children of the Damned: The ruins of St. Dunstan-in-the-East, St. Dunstans Hill, London, features in the climax of the movie. (Photograph by the author.)

The Comeback
Enterprise (1977)

Cast: Jack Jones, Sheila Keith, Pamela Stephenson, David Doyle, Bill Owen, Richard Johnson, Holly Palance
Screenplay: Murray Smith
Producer-Director: Pete Walker

An American singer trying to make a comeback is drawn into a series of gruesome murders.

Top: A Clockwork Orange: Northern Subway, Trinity Road, Wandsworth, London, features in the opening sequence in which the droogs beat up an old tramp. (Photograph by the author.) *Bottom: A Clockwork Orange*: Doubling as the Woodmere Health Farm is Manor Lodge School, Ridge Hill, Shenley, Hertfordshire. Courtesy of Ruth Potter.

The Comeback: Featuring as Foxwarren House, the home of Mr. and Mrs. B. (Bill Owen & Sheila Keith), is "Foxwarren," Redhill Road, Cobham, Surrey. Courtesy of Simon Flynn.

Location: Foxwarren House (exterior and interior): "Foxwarren," Foxwarren Park, Redhill Road, Cobham, Surrey.

Foxwarren, a large and quite striking private house, is actually named Foxwarren in the movie, and is the home of Sheila Keith and Bill Owen (Mr. & Mrs. B).

Count Dracula
BBC Films (1977)

Cast: Louis Jourdan, Frank Finlay, Susan Penhaligon, Judi Bowker, Jack Shepherd, Mark Burns, Bosco Hogan
Screenplay: Gerald Savory
Producer: Morris Barry
Director: Philip Saville

The Transylvanian vampire count gets his comeuppance in Yorkshire.

Location: Castle Dracula (exterior only): Alnwick Castle, Alnwick, Northumberland, NE66 1NQ.
Whitby Town: Whitby, North Yorkshire.

Doubling as Castle Dracula is Alnwick Castle in Northumberland (see the chapter "Locations — In Detail" for a more in-depth look). For the first time in any Dracula film production, the fishing town of Whitby in North Yorkshire does actually double as Whitby, as written in the novel by Bram Stoker.

Craze
Harbour Productions (1974)

Cast: Jack Palance, Julie Ege, Trevor Howard, Diana Dors, Suzy Kendall, Michael Jayston, Edith Evans, Hugh Griffith, Percy Herbert, Kathleen Byron, David Warbeck, Marianne Stone
Screenplay: Aben Kandel, Herman Cohen
Producer: Herman Cohen
Director: Freddie Francis

An antique dealer makes human sacrifices to an African idol when he discovers that it will bring him wealth in exchange.

Studio: Shepperton Studios, Middlesex.
Location: Aunt Louise's House (exterior): Thorpe House, TASIS (The American School in England), Coldharbour Lane, Thorpe, Surrey, TW20 8TE.

See the chapter "Locations — In Detail" for an in-depth look at Thorpe House, which appears here briefly as the home of Aunt Louise (Edith Evans), who is sacrificed in her own garden by her evil nephew, Jack Palance.

The exterior of the antique shop in the film was a set built on the back lot at Shepperton Studios.

Creep
Dan Films (2004)

Cast: Franka Potente, Vas Blackwood, Ken Campbell, Jeremy Sheffield, Paul Rattray, Kelly Scott, Sean Harris
Producer: Julie Baines, Jason Newmark
Screenplay-Director: Christopher Smith

Trapped on the London underground, a young woman is stalked by a vicious psycho.

Location: London Underground: Charing Cross.

All London underground platform sequences featuring Franka Potente were filmed at Charing Cross, which can be found on the Northern Line.

The Creeping Flesh: The Victorian home of Emmanuel Hildern (Peter Cushing) is Thorpe House, Coldharbour Lane, Thorpe, Surrey. Courtesy of Simon Flynn.

The Creeping Flesh
World Film Services (1972)

Cast: Christopher Lee, Peter Cushing, Lorna Heilbron, George Benson, Kenneth J. Warren, Duncan Lamont, Michael Ripper, Catherine Finn, David Bailie, Marianne Stone
Screenplay: Peter Spenceley, Jonathan Rumbold
Producer: Michael Redbourn
Director: Freddie Francis

A Victorian scientist discovers that water causes the recomposing of tissue on the skeleton on a Neanderthal man.

Studio: Shepperton Studios, Middlesex.
Location: Emmanuel Hildern's House (exterior): Thorpe House, TASIS (The American School in England), Coldharbour Lane, Thorpe, Surrey, TW20 8TE.

Doubling as the Victorian home of Emmanuel Hildern (Peter Cushing) is Thorpe House, where, in a creepy climax, the creeping flesh stalks Cushing. The scene includes a beautifully shot night sequence of the monster's shadow slowly walking toward the front door.

Crucible of Terror
Glendale (1971)

Cast: Mike Raven, Mary Maude, James Bolam, Ronald Lacey, John Arnatt, Beth Morris, Judy Matheson, Melissa Stribling
Screenplay: Ted Hooker, Tom Parkinson
Producer: Tom Parkinson
Director: Ted Hooker

A mad sculptor murders his beautiful models, then covers them in wax before casting them in bronze.

Studio: Shepperton Studios, Middlesex.
Location: Jericho Valley: St. Agnes, Cornwall.

St. Agnes is a beautiful, picturesque village on the north Cornwall coast, and doubles here as Jericho Valley, the home of mad sculptor Victor (Mike Raven).

Crucible of Terror: Doubling as Jericho Valley is the beautiful picture postcard, St. Agnes, Cornwall. (Photograph by the author.)

Cry of the Banshee
American International Pictures (1970)

Cast: Vincent Price, Elisabeth Bergner, Essy Persson, Hugh Griffith, Hilary Dwyer, Sally Geeson, Robert Hutton, Patrick Mower, Carl Rigg, Godfrey James
Screenplay: Tim Kelly, Christopher Wicking
Producer-Director: Gordon Hessler

A sixteenth century witch curses a magistrate and sends a devil after him to exact her revenge.

Locations: The House of Whitman (exterior and interior): Grim's Dyke Hotel, Old Redding, Harrow Weald, London, HA3 6SH.

Nearly the entire film was shot on location at Grim's Dyke, using both the interior and exterior for the Elizabethan home of evil magistrate Lord Edward Whitman (Vincent Price), haunted by the evil spirit of Roderick (Patrick Mower).

The Curse of Frankenstein
Hammer Films (1957)

Cast: Peter Cushing, Christopher Lee, Hazel Court, Robert Urquhart, Valerie Gaunt, Noel Hood, Melvyn Hayes, Sally Walsh, Fred Johnson
Screenplay: Jimmy Sangster
Producer: Anthony Hinds
Director: Terence Fisher

Baron Frankenstein creates a living monster from corpses, and it goes on the rampage.

Studio: Bray Studios, Windsor, Berkshire.
Location: Chateau Frankenstein (exterior): Oakley Court Hotel, Windsor Road, Water Oakley, Windsor, SL4 5UR.

The exterior of Oakley Court is seen in several night shots as the towering Chateau Frankenstein.
The Curse of Frankenstein was the first true Hammer horror film and the first British horror film to be shot in glorious Technicolor; Hammer made sure that they threw in lots of blood and gore for good measure.
This was also the film that made overnight stars of both Peter Cushing and Christopher Lee.

The Curse of the Crimson Altar
Tigon Films (1968)

Cast: Boris Karloff, Christopher Lee, Rupert Davies, Mark Eden, Barbara Steele, Michael Gough, Virginia Wetherell
Screenplay: Mervyn Haisman, Henry Lincoln
Producer: Tony Tenser
Director: Vernon Sewell

An English country lodge is the setting for a mixture of witchcraft and mystery.

Location: Craxted Lodge (exterior and interior): Grim's Dyke Hotel, Old Redding, Harrow Weald, London, HAR 6SH.

Both the interior and exterior of Grim's Dyke were used for the film, doubling as Craxted Lodge, the home of, Morley (Christopher Lee). The movie gives us one of the final screen performances of Boris Karloff, playing Professor John Marshe.

The Curse of the Crimson Altar: Grim's Dyke Hotel, Harrow Weald, London, features as Craxted Lodge, the home of Morley (Christopher Lee). (Photograph by the author.)

The Dark Eyes of London
Pathe (1939)

Cast: Bela Lugosi, Hugh Williams, Greta Gynt, Wilfrid Walter, Edmon Ryan
Screenplay: John Argyle, Walter Summers, Patrick Kirwan
Producer: John Argyle
Director: Walter Summers

The proprietor of a home for the blind uses a mute giant to drown insured victims.

Studio: Welwyn Film Studios, Welwyn-Garden-City, Hertfordshire.
Location: London (opening credits): Tower Bridge, Tower Hill, London, SE1 2UP.

Dark Eyes of London: Setting the London scene at the opening of the film is Tower Bridge, Tower Hill, London. (Photograph by the author.)

This was Bela Lugosi's second film on British soil, with all of his scenes shot on sound stages at Welwyn Film Studios in Hertfordshire.

During the opening credits, Tower Bridge, one of the world's most famous and recognizable bridges, completed after eight years of construction in 1884, sets the London scene.

As a note of interest, it was the first British film to be given an H (for Horror) certificate.

Now largely forgotten, Welwyn Film Studios opened in 1928, and its main output was second features. It was not on the same scale as other film studios of the time, and so it closed in the 1950s.

Dead of Night
Ealing (1945)

Cast: Mervyn Johns, Roland Culver, Anthony Baird, Sally Ann Howes, Frederick Valk, Googie Withers, Basil Radford, Miles Malleson, Michael Redgrave

Screenplay: John Baines, Angus MacPhail, T.E.B. Clarke

Producers: Michael Balcon, Sidney Cole, John Croydon

Director: Cavalcanti, Charles Crichton, Robert Hamer, Basil Dearden

An architect is caught up in a recurring series of macabre dreams.

Studio: Ealing Studios, London
Location: Golfing Wedding: St. Mary the Virgin, Church Walk, Weston Turville, Aylesbury, Buckinghamshire, HP22 5SH.

Featured as the church in the golfing wedding sequence is the thirteenth century St. Mary the Virgin in Weston Turville, Buckinghamshire. *Dead of Night*, was the first British compendium horror film.

Death Line
Harbor Ventures (1972)

Cast: Donald Pleasence, David Ladd, Sharon Gurney, Christopher Lee, Norman Rossington, James Cossins, Clive Swift, Hugh Armstrong
Screenplay: Ceri Jones
Producer: Paul Maslansky
Director: Gary Sherman

A strange, cannibalistic being lives in the bowels of the London Underground system.

Location: London Underground: Russell Square.

All London underground platform sequences featuring the vicious, yet sad, man turned cannibal (played very powerfully by Hugh Armstrong) were filmed at Russell Square, which can be found on the Piccadilly line.

Demons of the Mind
Hammer Films (1972)

Cast: Paul Jones, Patrick Magee, Gillian Hills, Robert Hardy, Michael Hordern, Shane Briant, Yvonne Mitchell, Kenneth J. Warren, Virginia Wetherell
Screenplay: Christopher Wicking

Dead of Night: The golfing wedding sequence was shot on location at St. Mary the Virgin, Church Walk, Weston Turville, Aylesbury, Buckinghamshire. (Photograph by the author.)

Producer: Frank Godwin
Director: Peter Sykes

A baron keeps his son and daughter as virtual prisoners, for he is convinced that insanity runs in the family.

Studio: Elstree Studios, Borehamwood, Hertfordshire.
Location: Baron Zom's Chateau (exterior and interior): Wykehurst Place, Wykehurst Park, Bolney, West Sussex.

Featuring here as the very impressive home of Baron Zom (Robert Hardy) is Wykehurst Place in West Sussex. See the chapter "Wykehurst Place" for a more in-depth look.

The Descent
Celador Films (2005)

Cast: Shauna Macdonald, Natalie Mendoza, Alex Reid, Saskia Mulder, Nora-Jane Noone, Myanna Buring, Oliver Miburn
Producer: Christian Colson
Screenplay-Director: Neil Marshall

Six young women on a caving holiday find themselves trapped underground with a race of cannibalistic predators.

Studio: Pinewood Studios, Buckinghamshire.
Locations: Appalachian Mountains: Pitlochry, Tayside, Scotland.
Log Cabin (exterior and interior): The Shooting Lodge, Ashridge Estate, Moneybury Hill, Ringshall, Berkhamsted, Hertfordshire, HP4 1LX.

Doubling as America's Appalachian Mountains, where the women go caving, is Pitlochry in Scotland with its miles of beautifully scenic forests.

The log cabin where the group stays is The Shooting Lodge, a National Trust property on the Ashridge Estate in Hertfordshire. This is parkland, and open to the public.

The interior of the cave is actually huge set pieces which were built on sound stages at Pinewood Studios.

The Devil Rides Out
Hammer Films (1968)

Cast: Christopher Lee, Charles Gray, Leon Greene, Patrick Mower, Gwen Ffrangcon-Davies, Sarah Lawson, Paul Eddington
Screenplay: Richard Matheson
Producer: Anthony Nelson-Keys

The Devil Rides Out: Edgwarebury Corus Hotel, Barnet Lane, Elstree, Borehamwood, Hertfordshire, doubles as the home of Richard (Paul Eddington). Courtesy of Ruth Potter.

Director: Terence Fisher

The duc de Richleau rescues a friend from a group of Satanists.

Studio: Elstree Studios, Borehamwood, Hertfordshire.
Location: Richard's House (exterior): Edgwarebury Corus Hotel, Barnet Lane, Elstree, Borehamwood, Hertfordshire, WD6 3RE.
Mocata's House (exterior): High Canons, Buckettsland Lane, Well End, Hertfordshire, WD6 5PL.

See chapter "Locations — In Detail" for a more in-depth look at the Edgwarebury Corus Hotel, which features in the movie as the home of, Richard Eaton (Paul Eddington). High Cannons, a large private country house is the home, of devil worshipper Mocata (Charles Gray).

Die Monster Die!
American International Pictures (1965)

Cast: Boris Karloff, Nick Adams, Freda Jackson, Suzan Farmer, Patrick Magee, Harold Goodwin, Sydney Bromley

Screenplay: Jerry Sohl
Producer: Pat Green
Director: Daniel Haller

An English scientist hides a meteorite that causes humans to mutate and plants to grow huge in size.

Studio: Shepperton Studios, Middlesex.
Location: The Witley Place (exterior): Oakley Court Hotel, Windsor Road, Water Oakley, Windsor, SL4 5UR.

The exterior of Oakley doubles as the home of Nahum Witley (Boris Karloff).

Dr. Terror's House of Horrors
Amicus Films (1965)

Cast: Peter Cushing, Christopher Lee, Ursula Howells, Peter Madden, Max Adrian, Roy Castle, Alan Freeman, Bernard Lee, Jeremy Kemp, Kenny Lynch, Michael Gough, Donald Sutherland
Screenplay: Milton Subotsky
Producers: Milton Subotsky, Max J. Rosenberg
Director: Freddie Francis

An eccentric, who turns out to be Death himself, tells the fortunes of five men in a railway carriage.

Studio: Shepperton Studios, Middlesex.
Location: Bradley Train Station (opening sequence): King's Cross Station, King's Cross, London, N1.

Due to budget restrictions, most of the film was shot on sound stages and on the back lot at Shepperton Studios. However, part of the opening train station sequence (the fictional Bradley Station) was shot on location at King's Cross Station in London. This was the first of the Amicus compendium pictures.

Doomwatch
Tigon Films (1972)

Cast: Ian Bannen, Judy Geeson, George Sanders, Percy Herbert, Geoffrey Keen, Joseph O'Conor, George Woodbridge
Screenplay: Clive Exton
Producer: Tony Tenser
Director: Peter Sasdy

The inhabitants of a remote island are being affected by a strange disease, caused by the illegal dumping of nuclear waste.

Studio: Pinewood Studios, Buckinghamshire.
Location: Balfe Island: Polperro, Cornwall.

The remote Balfe Island, where Ian Bannen and Judy Geeson find themselves, is actually the picture book village of Polperro in Cornwall, with its narrow winding streets and cottages perched on steep slopes overlooking a tiny harbor.

Dracula
Hammer Films (1958)

Cast: Peter Cushing, Christopher Lee, Michael Gough, Melissa Stribling, Carol Marsh, Valerie Gaunt, John Van Eyssen, Miles Malleson, George Benson, Charles Lloyd Pack, Geoffrey Bayldon
Screenplay: Jimmy Sangster
Producer: Anthony Hinds
Director: Terence Fisher

Arguably the best film version of all the screen adaptations of Stoker's classic novel.

Studio: Bray Studios, Windsor, Berkshire.

All of the beautiful interiors for the film were built on sound stages at Bray Studios. The authentic-looking exterior of Castle Dracula was a set built at Bray. All were the handiwork of Hammer's fabulous artistic director, Bernard Robinson.

Dracula
Dan Curtis Production (1973)

Cast: Jack Palance, Simon Ward, Nigel Davenport, Pamela Brown, Fiona Lewis, Penelope Horner, Murray Brown, Virginia Wetherell, George Pravda, Eddie Powell
Screenplay: Richard Matheson
Producer-Director: Dan Curtis

After he attacks the lovely Lucy Westenra, the centuries-old vampire Count Dracula is threatened by Dr. Van Helsing, and a spine-tingling hunt for the blood-sucker ensues.

Location: Carfax (interior and exterior): Oakley Court Hotel, Windsor Road, Water Oakley, Windsor, SL4 5UR.

Oakley was an excellent choice to double as Carfax, the English home of Count Dracula, played in a rather different (yet entertaining) style by Jack Palance.

Dracula
Universal Pictures (1979)

Cast: Frank Langella, Laurence Olivier, Kate Nelligan, Donald Pleasence, Trevor Eve, Jan Francis, Tony Haygarth, Teddy Turner, Sylvester McCoy
Screenplay: W.D. Richter
Producers: Martin Mirisch, Tom Pevsner
Director: John Badham

A Transylvanian count travels to Whitby and unleashes a wave of terror.

Studio: Shepperton Studios, Middlesex.
Locations: Castle Dracula (exterior): St. Michael's Mount, Marazion, Cornwall TR17 OEF.
Seward Institute (exterior and interior): Camelot Castle, Tintagel, Cornwall, PL34 0DQ.

Dracula (1979): Doubling as Castle Dracula during the opening credits is St. Michael's Mount, Marazion, Cornwall. (Photograph by the author.)

Dracula (1979): Featured throughout the film as the home of Dr. Jack Seward (Donald Pleasence) is Camelot Castle, Tintagel, Cornwall. Courtesy of Kate Holland.

Castle Dracula, which features briefly in a dramatic opening credit sequence, is St. Michael's Mount, Cornwall, which is part Benedictine Priory, and part medieval castle (see "Locations — In Detail" for a more in-depth look).

Doubling as the home of Dr. Jack Seward (Donald Pleasence), and used in many dramatic and highly effective sequences featuring Pleasence, Laurence Olivier and Frank Langella (Count Dracula), is Camelot Castle in Cornwall (see "Locations — In Detail").

Dracula A.D. 1972
Hammer Films (1971)

Cast: Peter Cushing, Christopher Lee, Stephanie Beacham, Michael Coles, William Ellis, Christopher Neame, Marsha Hunt, Michael Kitchen, Caroline Munro, Janet Key, Lally Bowers
Screenplay: Don Houghton
Producer: Josephine Douglas
Director: Alan Gibson

Dracula reappears among Chelsea teenagers practicing black magic.

Dracula A.D. 1972: Tykes Water Lake & Bridge, Aldenham Road, Elstree, Hertfordshire, features during the pre-credit sequence. (Photograph by the author.)

Dracula A.D. 1972: Hadley Common, Barnet, London, can be seen during the pre-credit sequence, featuring Dracula (Christopher Lee) and Van Helsing (Peter Cushing). Courtesy of Ruth Potter.

Studio: Elstree Studios, Borehamwood, Hertfordshire.

Locations: Pre-Credit Sequence Featuring Dracula and Van Helsing: Tykes Water Lake & Bridge, Haberdashers' Aske's School for Girls, Aldenham Road, Elstree, Hertfordshire, WD6 3BT and Hadley Common, Barnet, London.

Cavern (interior and exterior): Pizza Rock, 372 King's Road, Chelsea, London.

Tykes Water Lake & Bridge (private except for permitted fisherman) and the not-so-private Hadley Common, an open space used by walkers, are both seen at the opening of the film, when Dracula (Christopher Lee) and Van Helsing (Peter Cushing) are fighting to the death atop a horse-drawn carriage.

The cavern with its webbed, cavern-like interior, where Stephanie Beacham, Caroline Munro, Christopher Neame and co. meet up, is today a pizza restaurant at 372 King's Road in London.

Tykes Water Lake & Bridge can be seen in several other horror movies, including *Taste the Blood of Dracula*, *The Abominable Dr. Phibes*, *Fear in the Night* and *The Monster Club*.

Dracula A.D. 1972: Doubling as the Cavern is Pizza Rock, 372 King's Road, Chelsea, London. (Photograph by the author.)

Dracula Has Risen from the Grave
Hammer Films (1968)

Cast: Christopher Lee, Rupert Davies, Veronica Carlson, Barbara Ewing, Barry Andrews, Ewan Hooper, Michael Ripper, George A. Cooper
Screenplay: John Elder
Producer: Aida Young
Director: Freddie Francis

Count Dracula pursues the pretty niece of a small-town priest.

Studio: Pinewood Studios, Buckinghamshire.
Location: Woodland: Black Park, Black Park Road, Wexham, Buckinghamshire, SL3 6DR.

Seen throughout the film, and in several scenes featuring Christopher Lee (Count Dracula) riding in a speeding horse-drawn carriage, is Black Park.

Dream Demon
Palace Pictures (1988)

Cast: Jemma Redgrave, Kathleen Wilhoite, Jimmy Nail, Timothy Spall, Annabelle Lanyon, Susan Fleetwood, Mark Green Street, Nickolas Grace, Richard Warner
Screenplay: Harley Cokliss, Christopher Wicking
Producer: Paul Webster
Director: Harley Cokliss

A rich heiress, about to be married, suffers from horrific nightmares that draw her into a world where reality and dreams meet.

Location: Diana's House (exterior): 53 Eton Avenue, Hampstead, London, NW3.

Featured as the home of Diana (Jemma Redgrave) is 53 Eton Avenue, a large private house in Hampstead. It is seen throughout the movie and in several prominent scenes with Jimmy Nail and Timothy Spall.

Dream Demon: Doubling as the home of Diana (Jemma Redgrave) is 53 Eton Avenue, Hampstead, London. (Photograph by the author.)

Edge of Sanity
Allied Vision (1988)

Cast: Anthony Perkins, Glynis Barber, David Lodge, Sarah Maurthorp, Ben Cole, Lisa Davis, Kay Jewers, Harry Landis
Screenplay: J.P. Felix, Ron Raley
Producers: Edward Simons, Harry Alan Towers
Director: Gerard Kikoine

Dr. Jekyll, under the influence of drugs, becomes Jack the Ripper.

Location: Dr. Jekyll's House (exterior): 11 Crescent Grove, Clapham, London, SW4.

The house in which Dr. Jekyll (Anthony Perkins) lives with his wife (Glynis Barber) can be found at 11 Crescent Grove, a

Victorian-looking private estate in Clapham, just a step away from the hustle and bustle of modern London life.

The Elephant Man
Brooksfilms (1980)

Cast: Anthony Hopkins, John Hurt, John Gielgud, Anne Bancroft, Freddie Jones, Wendy Hiller, Michael Elphick, Hannah Gordon, John Standing, Lesley Dunlop, Kenny Baker, Roy Evans
Screenplay: Christopher de Vore, Eric Bergren, David Lynch
Producer: Stuart Cornfeld
Director: David Lynch

The beautifully made true-life story of a hideously deformed man, Joseph Merrick (The Elephant Man), who lived in a sometimes cruel Victorian England.

Studio: Shepperton Studios, Middlesex.

Left: Edge of Sanity: Featured as the home of Dr. Jekyll (Anthony Perkins) is 11 Crescent Grove, Clapham, London. (Photograph by the author.) *Right: The Elephant Man*: At the opening of the film, Frederick Treves (Anthony Hopkins) walks along grimy Victorian London streets in search of Joseph Merrick, the Elephant Man. One of the streets seen is Shad Thames, Butlers Wharf, Bermondsey, London. (Photograph by the author.)

The Elephant Man: The exterior of the London Hospital is the Royal Mint, Royal Mint Court, Tower Hill, London. (Photograph by the author.)

Locations: London Street: Shad Thames, Butlers Wharf, Bermondsey, London, SE1 and Clink Street, Southwark, London, SE1.

London Hospital (exterior): Royal Mint, Royal Mint Court, Tower Hill, London, EC3.

Carr Gomm's Office (interior): National Liberal Club, 1 Whitehall Court, Westminster, London, SW1.

Railway Station: Liverpool Street Station, Liverpool Street, Spitalfields, London, EC2.

Theatre (auditorium): Playhouse Theatre, Northumberland Avenue, London, WC2N 5DE.

I have never considered *The Elephant Man* a horror film. It is a deeply moving, highly emotional picture, expertly directed and superbly photographed (in black-and-white) by Freddie Francis. It was definitely one of his finest pieces of work but, sad to say, it was not nominated for an Oscar, which Freddie so richly deserved. I have included the film in this book because it most certainly has elements and scenes of a horrific nature.

At the opening of the film, Frederick Treves (Anthony Hopkins) is seen

The Elephant Man: The railway station sequence in which Joseph Merrick (John Hurt) is chased by a roaring mob was shot on location at Liverpool Street Station, Liverpool Street, Spitalfields, London. (Photograph by the author.)

walking along grimy Victorian London streets in search of Joseph Merrick (played beautifully by John Hurt). This was shot at both Shad Thames in Bermondsey, London, with its high, narrow passageways, and Clink Street in Southwark, London, behind Southwark Cathedral.

The old Royal Mint building, built in 1811, and standing across from the world-famous Tower of London, is the body permitted to manufacture coins in Great Britain. In the film it doubles as the exterior of the London Hospital where Merrick lived in his last years. In fact, Merrick's remains are still kept in a vault at the real London Hospital in Whitechapel.

Doubling as the office of Carr Gomm (John Gielgud) is the National Liberal Club in Westminster.

The railway station sequence in which Merrick is taunted by young children, and then chased by a roaring mob down into the toilets, was shot at the nineteenth century Liverpool Street Station in Spitalfields. The stations once-decayed Victorian splendor and wonderful gothic windows have in recent years been dramatically modernized, with many of its original features, including some of those seen in the film, being removed. It is in fact barely recognizable from the Liverpool Street Station of the 1980s, when David Lynch filmed there. As a note of interest, Liverpool Street Station is where the real Joseph Merrick arrived on his return from Brussels.

Doubling as the interior of the theatre where Merrick is invited by Mrs. Kendal (Anne Bancroft) is the Playhouse Theatre in London's West End.

Endless Night
British Lion (1971)

Cast: Hayley Mills, Hywel Bennett, Britt Ekland, George Sanders, Lois Maxwell, Peter Bowles, Patience Collier, Walter Gotell
Producer: Leslie Gilliat
Screenplay-Director: Sidney Gilliat

A chauffeur marries a rich American heiress and they move into a stately home only to find it turning into a nightmare mansion.

Locations: Fenella's Apartment (exterior): Chester Terrace, Regent's Park, London, NW1.

Mansion House (exterior): Grim's Dyke Hotel, Old Redding, Harrow Weald, London, HA3 6SH.

The apartment of Fenella (Hayley Mills) can be found on Chester Terrace in Regent's Park. Grim's Dyke Hotel in Harrow Weald, a familiar horror film location, doubles as the creepy mansion house to which Fenella moves with chauffeur Hywel Bennett.

Fear in the Night
Hammer Films (1971)

Cast: Judy Geeson, Joan Collins, Peter Cushing, Ralph Bates, Gillian Lind, James Cossins
Screenplay: Jimmy Sangster, Michael Syson
Producer-Director: Jimmy Sangster

A young woman recovering from a nervous breakdown is deluded into committing a murder.

Studio: Elstree Studios, Borehamwood, Hertfordshire.
Location: The School House (exterior and interior): Bhaktivedanta Manor, Hilfield Lane, Letchmore Heath, Aldenham, Watford, WD25 8EZ.

Built in 1884, Bhaktivedanta Manor, was originally called Piggots Manor. One of its owners was George Harrison of The Beatles, who gave it, as a gift, to the International Society for Krishna Consciousness; they immediately

Fear in the Night: Featuring as the sinister and isolated school house is Bhaktivedanta Manor, Hilfield Lane, Letchmore Heath, Aldenham, Watford. (Photograph by the author.)

renamed the property Bhaktivedanta (after the Society's founder). In the film it doubles as the sinister and isolated school house where Ralph Bates takes wife Judy Geeson and slowly tries to drive her crazy, with the help of his super-bitch lover, Joan Collins.

Today it is almost totally unchanged (both exterior and interior) from how it looks in the movie.

The Flesh and Blood Show
Tigon Films (1972)

Cast: Ray Brooks, Jenny Hanley, Luan Peters, Judy Matheson, Robin Askwith, Patrick Barr, Elizabeth Bradley, Raymond Young, Alan Curtis
Screenplay: Alfred Shaughnessy
Producer-Director: Pete Walker

Actors rehearsing a play in a derelict seaside theatre are killed off one by one.

Location: Seaside Theatre (exterior and interior): Pavilion Theatre, West Pier, Brighton, West Sussex.

The Flesh and Blood Show: Doubling as the derelict seaside theatre where a group of actors are murdered one by one is the Pavilion Theatre, West Pier, Brighton, West Sussex. The Pavilion was destroyed in a fire in 2003, and all that remains today is a metal framework. Courtesy of Simon Flynn.

Brighton's West Pier, which is Britain's only Grade 1–listed Pier, built between 1863 and 1866, caught fire in 2003 and, along with the 1,000-seat Pavilion Theatre, was totally destroyed. Today nothing more than a metal framework stands.

Frankenstein
Yorkshire Productions (1984)

Cast: Robert Powell, David Warner, Carrie Fisher, John Gielgud, Terence Alexander, Edward Judd
Producer: Bill Siegler
Screenplay-Director: Victor Gialanella

An obsessed scientist believes that he can resurrect the dead with the aid of massive electrical charges. When the experiment goes wrong, the result is a hideously burned creature which, in terrible pain and panic, escapes into the countryside.

Location: Castle Frankenstein (exterior and interior): Ripley Castle, Harrogate, North Yorkshire, HG3 3AY.

The home of Victor Frankenstein (Robert Powell) is "played" by Ripley Castle, which has been the Ingilby family seat since the 1300s. During the summertime, this splendid house and its beautiful grounds are open to the public.

Frankenstein and the Monster from Hell
Hammer Films (1972)

Cast: Peter Cushing, Shane Briant, Madeleine Smith, John Stratton, Bernard Lee, Dave Prowse, Patrick Troughton, Peter Madden, Sydney Bromley, Michael Ward, Charles Lloyd Pack, Norman Mitchell
Screenplay: John Elder
Producer: Roy Skeggs
Director: Terence Fisher

The baron turns an injured lunatic into a hairy ape man.

Studio: Elstree Studios, Borehamwood, Hertfordshire.
Location: Graveyard (opening sequence): Highgate Cemetery, Swain's Lane, London, N6 6PJ.

See the chapter "Locations — In Detail" for an in-depth look at Highgate, which features here at the opening of the film with a body snatcher (Patrick Troughton) digging up a fresh corpse, and then escaping from a police sergeant (Norman Mitchell) who catches him in the act.

Frankenstein Created Woman
Hammer Films (1966)

Cast: Peter Cushing, Thorley Walters, Susan Denberg, Robert Morris, Duncan Lamont, Derek Fowlds, Peter Madden, Peter Blythe, Barry Warren
Screenplay: John Elder
Producer: Anthony Nelson-Keys
Director: Terence Fisher

A cripple, Christina, is taunted to suicide after the wrongful execution of her lover. Baron Frankenstein gives her the body of a beautiful woman and the soul of her dear departed, and she plots to revenge herself on the real killers.

Studio: Bray Studios, Windsor, Berkshire.
Locations: Guillotine Site: Frensham Common, Frensham, Nr. Farnham, Surrey.
Woodland: Black Park, Black Park Road, Wexham, Buckinghamshire, SL3 6DR.

Frankenstein Created Woman: The guillotine sequences were filmed at Frensham Common, Nr. Farnham, Surrey. Courtesy of Simon Flynn.*

Frensham Common, a popular open space for public walks, is seen during the guillotine sequences featuring Robert Morris, Susan Denberg and Duncan Lamont. Black Park can be seen at the end of the film, when Susan Denberg (as Christina) fatally knifes Johann (Derek Fowlds).

Frankenstein Must Be Destroyed
Hammer Films (1969)

Cast: Peter Cushing, Simon Ward, Veronica Carlson, Maxine Audley, Thorley Walters, Freddie Jones, George Pravda, Geoffrey Bayldon, Peter Copley, Harold Goodwin, Frank Middlemass, Windsor Davies
Screenplay: Bert Batt
Producer: Anthony Nelson-Keys
Director: Terence Fisher

The baron transplants the brain of one colleague into the body of another, with disastrous results.

Studio: Elstree Studios, Borehamwood, Hertfordshire.

"Frensham is a vast area of common in the best part of Surrey. It is a very quiet and peaceful place of beauty."— Simon Flynn

Frankenstein Must Be Destroyed: Doubling as the Herzeg house is Stanmore Hall, Wood Lane, Stanmore, Middlesex. (Photograph by the author.)

Locations: The Herzeg House (exterior only): Stanmore Hall, Wood Lane, Stanmore, Middlesex, HA7.

Stanmore Hall (see the chapter "Locations — In Detail" for a more in-depth look), built in 1843 and originally a private house, was recently converted to apartments, with no access except for residents. It features here at the opening of the film, with Peter Cushing (as Baron Frankenstein) walking up the steps to the house, and then later, when the baron begins his chase to find the escaped Professor Richter (Freddie Jones).

Frankenstein: The True Story
Universal (1973)

Cast: James Mason, Leonard Whiting, David McCallum, Jane Seymour, Michael Sarrazin, Michael Wilding, Margaret Leighton, Ralph Richardson, John Gielgud, Tom Baker, Arnold Diamond, Yootha Joyce, Norman Rossington
Screenplay: Don Bachardy, Christopher Isherwood
Producer: Hunt Stromberg Jr.
Director: Jack Smight

A more psychological telling of the Mary Shelley story, with a different kind of monster.

Studio: Pinewood Studios, Buckinghamshire.

Locations: The Fanshawe House (exterior): Cliveden House Hotel, Taplow, Buckinghamshire, SL6 OJF.

The Fanshawe House (interior): Blenheim Palace, Woodstock, Oxfordshire, OX20 1PX.

Victor Frankenstein's Lodgings (exterior only): The Lych Gate, Vicarage Walk, Bray, Berkshire, SL6 2AE.

The home of the Fanshawes is the very impressive seventeenth century Cliveden House, a hotel in a beautiful country home setting (see the chapter "Locations — In Detail" for a more in-depth look).

The Fanshawe house interiors were filmed at Blenheim Palace in Oxfordshire, a lavish eighteenth century manor and the birthplace of Sir Winston Churchill (see the chapter "Locations — In Detail" for a more in-depth look).

The Lych Gate, an unusual fifteenth century gatehouse at St. Michael's Church in Bray, doubles at the lodgings of Victor Frankenstein (Leonard Whiting).

Frenzy
Universal Pictures (1972)

Cast: Jon Finch, Alec McGowen, Barry Foster, Barbara Leigh-Hunt, Anna Massey, Vivien Merchant, Bernard Cribbins, Billie Whitelaw, Michael Bates, Clive Swift, Jean Marsh

Screenplay: Anthony Shaffer

Producer-Director: Alfred Hitchcock

A crazed killer uses neckties to strangle his women victims.

Studio: Pinewood Studios, Buckinghamshire.

Locations: London (opening credits): Tower Bridge, London, SE1 2UP.

The Globe (interior and exterior): The Globe, 37 Bow Street, Covent Garden, London, WC2.

Frenzy: The flat where Robert Rusk (Barry Foster) lives is at 3 Henrietta Street, Covent Garden, London. (Photograph by the author.)

Frenzy: "The Globe," 37 Bow Street, Covent Garden, London, is the public house owned by the character, Forsythe (Bernard Cribbins). (Photograph by the author.)

Robert Rusk's Flat (exterior): 3 Henrietta Street, Covent Garden, London, WC2.

To set the London scene during the opening credits, the camera glides over the Thames toward one of London's most famous tourist attractions, Tower Bridge.

The Globe public house in Covent Garden, almost unchanged since Hitchcock filmed there, is the pub in the movie owned by Forsythe (Bernard Cribbins), who sacks worker Blaney (Jon Finch), a murder suspect.

Robert Rusk's (Barry Foster) flat is also in Covent Garden, and can be found at 3 Henrietta Street, which features in the very famous sequence in which the camera moves slowly down the staircase from Rusk's apartment and out into the busy street.

Frightmare
Heritage (1974)

Cast: Rupert Davies, Sheila Keith, Deborah Fairfax, Paul Greenwood, Kim Butcher, Fiona Curzon, Andrew Sachs, Leo Genn, Gerald Flood

Frightmare: Doubling as the home of Edmund (Rupert Davies) and Dorothy Yates (Sheila Keith) is Dawes Farm, Fernhurst, Nr. Haslemere, West Sussex. Courtesy of Simon Flynn.*

Screenplay: David McGillivray
Producer-Director: Pete Walker

Edmund and Dorothy Yates are released after fifteen years in a mental asylum, and Dorothy starts committing her hideous cannibalistic crimes once again.

Location: The Yates Farmhouse (exterior and interior): Dawes Farm, Henley Common, Fernhurst, Nr. Haslemere, West Sussex, GU27 3HB.

Dawes Farm, an ordinary looking farmhouse, hides an horrific secret: It doubled as the home of Edmund (Rupert Davies) and Dorothy Yates (Sheila Keith), a lady who is doing some very nasty cranial D.I.Y.

From Beyond the Grave
Amicus Films (1972)

Cast: Peter Cushing, David Warner, Donald Pleasence, Ian Bannen, Diana Dors, Margaret Leighton, Ian Carmichael, Nyree Dawn Porter, Ian Ogilvy, Lesley-Anne Down, Angela Pleasence, Jack Watson

"Looking through the leaded windows I expected to see Sheila Keith dealing out her tarot cards to some doomed visitor."—Simon Flynn

From Beyond the Grave: The creepy cemetery seen during the opening credits is Highgate Cemetery, Swain's Lane, London. Courtesy of Elmar Podlasly.

Screenplay: Robin Clarke, Raymond Christodoulou
Producer: Milton Subotsky
Director: Kevin Connor

The proprietor of an East End antique shop involves his customers in horrific situations.

Studio: Shepperton Studios, Middlesex.
Location: Graveyard (opening credits sequence): Highgate Cemetery, Swain's Lane, London, N6 6PJ.

Used to splendid gothic effect during the opening credits is Highgate Cemetery, with mist swirling around its many mausoleums, vaults and catacombs.

The antique shop in the film — Temptations Ltd. — has long been believed to be a real antique shop in London, but it was just a set built on the back lot at Shepperton.

Funny Man
Nomad Pictures (1994)

Cast: Tim James, Christopher Lee, Benny Young, Pauline Chan, Ingrid Lacy, Matthew Devitt, Chris Walker, Ed Bishop
Producer: Nigel Odell
Screenplay-Director: Simon Sprackling

When Max Taylor wins a mansion house of Callum Chance in a game of poker, little does he realize that the game is far from over, as one by one his family are murdered by the Funny Man, a demonic jester.

Studio: Shepperton Studios, Middlesex.
Location: The Chance Manor (exterior and interior): Wyfold Court, Rotherfield Peppard, Henley-on-Thames, Oxfordshire, RG9 5WF.

The Grade II Victorian mansion house, Wyfold Court, in Oxfordshire doubles as the ancestral home of Chance (Christopher Lee).

The Ghoul
Gaumont British (1933)

Cast: Boris Karloff, Cedric Hardwicke, Ralph Richardson, Kathleen Harrison, Ernest Thesiger, Anthony Bushell
Screenplay: Frank King, Leonard Hines, L. DuGarde Peach, Roland Pertwee, John Hastings Turner, Rupert Downing
Producer: Michael Balcon
Director: T. Hayes Hunter

An Egyptologist returns from the tomb to uncover stolen jewels and a murderer.

Studio: Lime Grove Studios, Lime Grove, Shepherd's Bush, London.

This horror film, featuring the already immortalized horror movie legend Boris Karloff (making his first British horror film appearance), was shot entirely at Lime Grove Studios, which is now sadly demolished.

The Ghoul
Tyburn Productions (1974)

Cast: Peter Cushing, Alexandra Bastedo, John Hurt, Gwen Watford, Veronica Carlson, Don Henderson, Ian McCulloch, Stewart Bevan, Dan Meaden
Screenplay: John Elder

The Ghoul (1974): The party sequence at the opening of the film was shot at Heatherden Hall, Pinewood Studios, Iver Heath, Buckinghamshire. (Photograph by the author.)

Producer: Kevin Francis
Director: Freddie Francis

A group of travelers are attacked by something that lurks in the house of a former clergyman.

Studio: Pinewood Studios, Buckinghamshire.
Location: Party Site: Heatherden Hall, Pinewood Studios, Iver Heath, Buckinghamshire, SL0 ONH.

Nearly the entire film was shot on sound stages at Pinewood Studios. However, the opening party sequence was shot both exterior and interior at Heatherden Hall, which stands in the grounds at Pinewood.

Gothic
Virgin Vision (1986)

Cast: Gabriel Byrne, Julian Sands, Natasha Richardson, Timothy Spall, Miriam Cyr
Screenplay: Stephen Volk
Producer: Penny Corke

Gothic: Featuring throughout the film as the chateau of Lord Byron (Gabriel Byrne) is Gaddesden Place, Great Gaddesden, Hemel Hempstead, Hertfordshire. (Photograph by the author.)

Director: Ken Russell

A recreation of the night in 1816 when Mary Shelley and Dr. Polidori were inspired to write their gothic horror classics Frankenstein and The Vampyre.

Location: Villa Diodati (exterior and interior): Gaddesden Place, Great Gaddesden, Hemel Hempstead, Hertfordshire, HP2 6EX.

Gaddesden Place, built between 1768 and 1773, and overlooking some of the most beautiful countryside in England, features throughout the film as the home of Lord Byron (Gabriel Byrne), who takes his guests, Percy Shelley (Julian Sands) and Mary Shelley (Natasha Richardson), into the darker sides of their imaginations.

Half Light
United International Pictures (2006)

Cast: Demi Moore, Henry Ian Cusick, Kate Isitt, Nicholas Gleaves, James Cosmo, Joanna Hole, Therese Bradley, Hans Matheson

62 Half Light

Half Light: Doubling as Ingonish Cove where Demi Moore is spooked by the locals is the eighteenth century fishing village Porth Dinllaen, Llleyn Peninsula, Gwynedd, Wales. Courtesy of Alan Hughes.

Producers: Garth H. Drabinsky, Joel B. Michaels, Clive Parsons, Steve Samuels, Andreas Schmid
Screenplay-Director: Craig Rosenberg

When Rachel Carlson moves to a remote Scottish coastal village after the death of her son, strange things start to happen when she is haunted by ghosts and real life terror.

Studio: Ealing Studios, London.
Locations: Village of Ingonish Cove: Porth Dinllaen, Lleyn Peninsula, Gwynedd, Wales.
Church (exterior and interior): St. Patrick's Church, Llanbadrig, Cemaes, Anglesey, Wales.

Preserved by the National Trust since 1994, and only reached by foot, Porth Dinllaen, an eighteenth century fishing village in Wales, doubles as the Scottish Ingonish Cove, where Rachel Carlson (Demi Moore) is spooked by the locals.

St. Patrick's Church, one of the oldest church sites in Anglesey, Wales, with its breathtaking cliff-edge location, features throughout the film.

Half Light: The unusual church with its graves perched high on a cliff is St. Patrick's Church, Llanbadrig, Cemaes, Anglesey, Wales. Courtesy of Alan Hughes.

Hands of the Ripper
Hammer Films (1971)

Cast: Eric Porter, Jane Merrow, Angharad Rees, Dora Bryan, Derek Godfrey, Lynda Baron, Norman Bird, Marjie Lawrence, Barry Lowe
Screenplay: L. W. Davidson
Producer: Aida Young
Director: Peter Sasdy

The daughter of Jack the Ripper grows up to become a murderess.

Studio: Pinewood Studios, Buckinghamshire.
Location: St. Paul's Cathedral (exterior): St. Paul's Cathedral, Ludgate Hill, London, EC4.

Hammer Films were not granted permission to shoot the climax of the film in the Whispering Gallery at St. Paul's Cathedral, and so they had to recreate the interior of St. Paul's at Pinewood Studios. They did a magnificent job, and one would think they filmed at the real place. Shooting of the exterior of St. Paul's was allowed, though (see the chapter "Locations — In Detail" for a more in-depth look).

Haunted
American Zoetrope (1995)

Cast: Aidan Quinn, Kate Beckinsale, Anthony Andrews, John Gielgud, Anna Massey, Geraldine Somerville, Liz Smith
Screenplay: Tim Prager, Lewis Gilbert, Bob Kellett
Producers: Anthony Andrews, Lewis Gilbert
Director: Lewis Gilbert

An academic who debunks psychic phenomena is invited by an old lady to visit a house which she claims is haunted.

Location: Edbrook Hall (interior and exterior): Parham House, Storrington, Nr. Pulborough, West Sussex, RH20 4HS.

See the chapter "Locations — In Detail" for an in-depth look at Parham House, which doubles here as Edbrook Hall, the haunted manor visited by academic and skeptic David Ash (Aidan Quinn).

Haunted House of Horror
Tigon Films (1969)

Cast: Frankie Avalon, Jill Hayworth, Dennis Price, Mark Wynter, George Sewell, Gina Warwick, Richard O'Sullivan, Robin Stewart, Clifford Earl
Screenplay: Michael Armstrong, Peter Marcus
Producer: Tony Tenser
Director: Michael Armstrong

Nasty things happen to a group of young people who spend the night in a haunted manor house.

Location: The Old Manor (exterior): Grim's Dyke Hotel, Old Redding, Harrow Weald, London, HA3 6SH.

Grim's Dyke doubles here as the haunted Old Manor.

The Haunting
Metro-Goldwyn-Mayer (1963)

Cast: Richard Johnson, Claire Bloom, Russ Tamblyn, Julie Harris, Valentine Dyall, Rosalie Crutchley
Screenplay: Nelson Gidding
Producer-Director: Robert Wise

An anthropologist, a skeptic and two mediums spend the weekend in a haunted mansion.

Haunted House of Horror: Doubling as the haunted old manor house is Grim's Dyke Hotel, Harrow Weald, London. Courtesy of Ruth Potter.

Studio: MGM Studios, Borehamwood, Hertfordshire.
Location: Hill House (exterior): Ettington Park Hotel, Alderminster, Stratford-upon-Avon, Warwickshire, CV37 8BU.

See the chapter "Locations — In Detail" for a more in-depth look at Ettington Park Hotel, which features here as Hill House, the haunted manor which slowly drives Eleanor (Julie Harris) to her death.

Ettington Park is beautifully photographed, giving off an air of true menace in glorious black-and-white. *The Haunting* is definitely one of the great haunted house pictures, proving that what you see is not as terrifying as what you *don't* see.

The Haunting
DreamWorks (1999)

Cast: Liam Neeson, Catherine Zeta-Jones, Owen Wilson, Lili Taylor, Bruce Dern
Screenplay: David Self
Producers: Susan Arnold, Donna Arkoff Roth, Colin Wilson

Director: Jan De Bont

When a group of people meet at a big, supposedly haunted house, terrible things start to occur.

Location: Hill House (exterior): Harlaxton Manor, Harlaxton, Grantham, Lincolnshire, NG32 1AG.

See the chapter "Locations — In Detail" for a more in-depth look at Harlaxton Manor, which doubles here perfectly as the haunted Hill House.

This film is not as powerful as the original, but does feature a nice performance from Lili Taylor (as Eleanor). However, the real star of the film is Halaxton, as no house could have been better chosen to play Hill House.

Hellraiser
New World Pictures (1987)

Cast: Andrew Robinson, Clare Higgins, Ashley Lawrence, Sean Chapman, Oliver Smith, Robert Hines, Doug Bradley

Producer: Christopher Figg
Screenplay-Director: Clive Barker

A woman tries to bring back her lover from the tortures of Hell by providing him with the blood of murder victims.

Location: Larry's House, the Mouth of Hell (exterior and interior): 187 Dollis Hill Lane, London, NW2.

Pinhead (Doug Bradley) first makes his appearance at 187 Dollis Hill Lane, a rather unusual-looking private house which stands out on a busy London street. Here it doubles as the home of Larry (Andrew Robinson).

Hellraiser: Doubling as the home of Larry (Andrew Robinson), where Pinhead (Doug Bradley) first makes his appearance, is 187 Dollis Hill Lane, London. (Photograph by the author.)

The Hole
Canal+ (2001)

Cast: Thora Birch, Desmond Harrington, Daniel Brocklebank, Laurence Fox, Keira Knightley, Embeth Davidtz

Screenplay: Ben Court, Caroline Ip
Producer: Lisa Bryer, Jeremy Bolt, Pippa Cross
Director: Nick Hamm

Four teenagers take a dare to be locked away in an old underground bunker. Their prank becomes a nightmare when the person who locked them there never returns.

Studio: Bray Studios, Windsor, Berkshire.
Location: Brabourne School (exterior and interior): Downside School and Abbey, Stratton-on-the-Fosse, Bath, BA3 4RJ.

Seen in the chilling opening sequence featuring Thora Birch, and then throughout the film, is the impressive-looking Downside School and Abbey, which was originally founded in the seventeenth century.

Horror Hospital
Noteworthy Films (1973)

Cast: Michael Gough, Robin Askwith, Vanessa Shaw, Dennis Price, Skip Martin
Screenplay: Antony Balch, Alan Watson
Producer: Richard Gordon
Director: Antony Balch

A songwriter goes to spend a week at a health hotel, run by a mysterious crippled doctor who gives lobotomies to all his patients.

Location: Dr. Storm's Health Hotel (exterior and interior): Knebworth House, Knebworth, Hertfordshire, SG3 6PY.

See the chapter "Locations — In Detail" for a more in-depth look at the impressive Knebworth House, seen here as Dr. Storm's Health Hotel (Michael Gough), where any visitor meets a horrific end.

The Hound of the Baskervilles
Hammer Films (1959)

Cast: Peter Cushing, Andre Morell, Christopher Lee, Marla Landi, Ewan Solon, Francis de Wolff, Miles Malleson, John Le Mesurier, Sam Kydd, David Oxley
Screenplay: Peter Bryan
Producer: Anthony Hinds
Director: Terence Fisher

The Hound of the Baskervilles: Frensham Common, Nr. Farnham, Surrey, doubles as the isolated Dartmoor. Courtesy of Simon Flynn.

Sherlock Holmes probes the case of a supernatural demonic hound that is said to bring death to an aristocratic family.

Studio: Bray Studios, Windsor, Berkshire.
Location: Dartmoor: Frensham Common, Frensham, Nr. Farnham, Surrey.

Frensham Common, a nature reserve in Surrey, was the perfect choice to double as the isolated Dartmoor, where Sherlock Holmes (Peter Cushing) and Doc Watson (Andre Morell) are pursued by a gigantic hound.

The House in Nightmare Park
Associated London Films (1972)

Cast: Frankie Howerd, Ray Milland, Hugh Burden, Kenneth Griffith, John Bennett, Rosalie Crutchley, Ruth Dunning
Screenplay-Producers: Clive Exton, Terry Nation
Director: Peter Sykes

A ham actor is asked to perform in an old dark house in the country, only to discover that a murderer is on the loose.

Studio: Shepperton Studios, Middlesex.

Location: Nightmare House (exterior): Oakley Court Hotel, Windsor Road, Water Oakley, Windsor, SL4 5UR.

Doubling as the old manor house where entertainer Foster Twelvetrees (Frankie Howerd) is invited to perform is Oakley Court.

House of Mortal Sin
Heritage (1975)

Cast: Anthony Sharp, Susan Penhaligon, Stephanie Beacham, Sheila Keith, Norman Eshley, Hilda Barry, Stuart Bevan, Mervyn Johns, Victor Winding, Andrew Sachs, Kim Butcher
Screenplay: David McGillivray
Producer-Director: Pete Walker

A sexually obsessed Catholic priest embarks on a career of blackmail and murder.

Location: Presbytery (exterior and interior): Waynflete Towers, Waynflete Tower Avenue, Esher, Surrey.

House of Mortal Sin: Featured as the Presbytery, the home of the evil Catholic priest (Anthony Sharp), is Waynflete Towers, Waynflete Tower Avenue, Esher, Surrey. Courtesy of Simon Flynn.*

Waynflete Towers doubles as the home of evil Catholic priest (Anthony Sharp) and an equally disturbed housekeeper (Sheila Keith).

House of the Long Shadows
Cannon Films (1982)

Cast: Vincent Price, Christopher Lee, Peter Cushing, John Carradine, Sheila Keith, Desi Arnaz, Jr., Julie Peasgood, Richard Todd, Louise English, Richard Hunter, Norman Rossington
Screenplay: Michael Armstrong
Producers: Menahem Golan, Yoram Globus
Director: Pete Walker

---

*"An unusually unique building at the bottom of an ordinary suburban road, full of houses (albeit posh houses, and they don't get much posher than Esher)." — Simon Flynn

House of the Long Shadows: Doubling as Baldpate Manor is Rotherfield House, East Tisted, Hampshire. Courtesy of Simon Flynn.*

An author goes to an isolated manor house to write a manuscript. Strange things start to happen as soon as he arrives.

Location: Baldpate Manor (interior and exterior): Rotherfield House, Rotherfield Park, East Tisted, Hampshire.

Doubling as Baldpate Manor is Rotherfield House, where nearly the entire movie was filmed, both interior and exterior, including some nicely photographed shadowy shots of the three titans of terror (Peter Cushing, Vincent Price and Christopher Lee) standing together. As a trio, they converged on screen here for the final time.

House of Whipcord
Heritage (1974)

Cast: Barbara Markham, Patrick Barr, Ray Brooks, Penny Irving, Anne Michelle, Sheila Keith, Dorothy Gordon, Robert Tayman, Judy Robinson
   Screenplay: David McGillivray
   Producer-Director: Pete Walker

*"There is an eerie mystery about this place. It is so isolated and looks completely empty. No sign of life in it at all. A monster all alone on top of a hill."—Simon Flynn

House of Whipcord: Littledean Jail, Littledean, Nr. Cinderford, Gloucestershire, doubles throughout the film as the rather unpleasant "House Of Correction." Courtesy of Sally-Anne Ryan.

> *A senile old judge and his vicious wife are so appalled by the decline in moral standards that they set up their own private house of correction for young girls.*

Location: House of Correction (exterior and interior): Littledean Jail, Littledean, Nr. Cinderford, Royal Forest of Dean, Gloucestershire, GL14 5NL.

See the chapter "Locations — In Detail" for a more in-depth look at Littledean Jail, which was the perfect double for the House of Correction, where Penny Irving is subjected to a horrific ordeal (locked up and beaten by the vicious warder, played by Sheila Keith).

The House That Dripped Blood
Amicus Films (1970)

Cast: Christopher Lee, Peter Cushing, Nyree Dawn Porter, John Bennett, Denholm Elliott, Tom Adams, Jon Pertwee, Ingrid Pitt, Chloe Franks, Joss Ackland, Geoffrey Bayldon, Wolfe Morris

Screenplay: Robert Bloch
Producers: Milton Subotsky, Max J. Rosenberg
Director: Peter Duffell

A detective investigates a disappearance in a sinister house that has a strange history.

Studio: Shepperton Studios, Middlesex.
Location: Jacquelin's Museum of Horror in the Segment "Waxworks" (exterior): Weybridge Hall, Church Street, Weybridge, Surrey, KT13 8DX.

In the segment "Waxworks," Peter Cushing and Joss Ackland become obsessed with a Museum Of Horror, which is actually Weybridge Hall in Surrey, standing totally unchanged since the time of the film.

Sadly the actual main house in the film — Yew Tree House — was a lodge on the back-lot at Shepperton, and was demolished in the early 1970s.

The Hunger
Metro-Goldwyn-Mayer (1983)

The Hunger: Doubling as the interior of Susan Sarandon's Park West clinic is Senate House, Malet Street, London. (Photograph by the author.)

Cast: Catherine Deneuve, Susan Sarandon, David Bowie, Cliff de Young, Willem Dafoe
Screenplay: Ivan Davis, Michael Thomas
Producer: Richard Shepherd
Director: Tony Scott

Two vampires live together in New York, and when one suddenly starts to age, the other is forced to try and find some way of helping him.

Studio: Shepperton Studios, Middlesex.
Locations: Opening Disco Sequence (interior): Heaven Nightclub, Villiers Street, London, WC2N 6NG.
Park West Clinic (interior): Senate House, Malet Street, London, WC1.

Heaven Nightclub, a vast gay complex under the arches at Charing Cross, was the interior of the disco in the opening sequence. While the interior of Susan Sarandon's Park West Clinic was shot at Senate House on Malet Street, London.

I Don't Want to Be Born
American International Pictures (1975)

Cast: Joan Collins, Ralph Bates, Donald Pleasence, Eileen Atkins, Caroline Munro, Hilary Mason, George Claydon
Screenplay: Stanley Price
Producer: Norma Corney
Director: Peter Sasdy

An ex-stripper gives birth to a monstrous baby which goes on a murderous rampage.

Studio: Pinewood Studios, Buckinghamshire.
Location: The Carlesi House (exterior and interior): 32 Wellington Square, Chelsea, London, SW3.

I Don't Want to Be Born: Doubling as the home of Lucy Carlesi (Joan Collins) is 32 Wellington Square, Chelsea, London. (Photograph by the author.)

32 Wellington Square, a very ordinary looking private house in London, features here as the home of Lucy Carlesi (Joan Collins), husband Gino (Ralph Bates), and their monstrous new born baby, that almost puts Damien Thorn in the shade.

The Innocents
20th Century–Fox (1961)

Cast: Deborah Kerr, Michael Redgrave, Peter Wyngarde, Megs Jenkins, Martin Stephens, Pamela Franklin
Screenplay: William Archibald, Truman Capote
Producer-Director: Jack Clayton

In Victorian times, a spinster governess in a lonely house finds her young charges possessed by evil demons of servants now dead.

Studio: Shepperton Studios, Middlesex.
Locations: Bly House (exterior): Sheffield Park House, Sheffield Park, East Sussex, TN22 3XQ.

The huge private neo–Gothic mansion Sheffield Park House (not accessible to the public) doubles as Bly House, where governess Deborah Kerr is haunted by evil spirits.

Cinematographer on the film was Freddie Francis, who considered this one of his best pieces of work.

Inseminoid
Jupiter Films (1980)

Cast: Robin Clarke, Jennifer Ashley, Stephanie Beacham, Steven Grives, Judy Geeson, Barry Houghton, Victoria Tennant, David Baxt
Screenplay: Nick Maley, Gloria Maley
Producers: Richard Gordon, David Speechley
Director: Norman J. Warren

Inseminoid: Chislehurst Caves, Old Hill, Chislehurst, Kent, doubles throughout the film as an underground space headquarters. (Photograph by the author.)

An alien creature takes over the body of a female member of a team of space archaeologists, and she gives birth to twin monsters.

Location: Underground Space Headquarters: Chislehurst Caves, Old Hill, Chislehurst, Kent, BR7 5NB.

See the chapter "Locations — In Detail" for a more in-depth look at Chislehurst Caves, which doubles as the Underground Space Headquarters of the group of archaeologists headed by Stephanie Beacham and Judy Geeson.

Interview with the Vampire
Warner Bros. (1994)

Cast: Tom Cruise, Brad Pitt, Antonio Banderas, Christian Slater, Stephen Rea, Kirsten Dunst, Roger Lloyd Pack
Screenplay: Anne Rice
Producers: Stephen Woolley, David Geffen
Director: Neil Jordan

A vampire reminisces about his life over the past 200 years and his enduring relationship with an older vampire.

Studio: Pinewood Studios, Buckinghamshire.
Location: Theatre Des Vampires (interior): Wilton's Music Hall, Graces Alley, Ensign Street, Whitechapel, London, E1.

The auditorium of the Theatre Des Vampires was actually a huge set built on a sound stage at Pinewood Studios, but some of the stage area is actually the auditorium of Wilton's Music Hall in Whitechapel. However, the music hall was heavily dressed with scenery, etc., making it almost unrecognizable.

Island of Terror
Planet Film Productions (1966)

Cast: Peter Cushing, Edward Judd, Carole Gray, Eddie Byrne, Sam Kydd, Niall MacGinnis, James Caffrey, Liam Gaffney, Peter Forbes Robertson
Screenplay: Edward Andrew Mann, Alan Ramsen
Producers: Tom Blakeley, Richard Gordon
Director: Terence Fisher

Hideous bone-eating monsters are loose on a remote Irish island.

Studio: Pinewood Studios, Buckinghamshire.
Location: Phillips's House (exterior): St. Huberts, St. Huberts Lane, Gerrards Cross, Buckinghamshire.

St. Huberts, a large private estate and house in Buckinghamshire, doubles as the manor house of Dr. Lawrence Phillips (Peter Forbes Robertson) where Brian Stanley (Peter Cushing) is attacked by a bone-eating monster.

Jack the Ripper
Euston Films (1988)

Cast: Michael Caine, Lewis Collins, Jane Seymour, Susan George, Lysette Anthony, Armand Assante, Ray McAnally, Ken Bones, Michael Gothard, Edward Judd, Harry Andrews, George Sweeney
Screenplay: Derek Marlowe, David Wickes
Producer-Director: David Wickes

In the Victorian London of 1888, the Ripper murders are finally attributed to a demented surgeon.

Studio: Pinewood Studios, Buckinghamshire.
Locations: London Street (opening credits): King Charles Street, Westminster, London, SW1.

Jack the Ripper: The huge Victorian Street seen during the opening credits is King Charles Street, Westminster, London. (Photograph by the author.)

Scotland Yard (exterior): Lincoln's Inn, Lincoln's Inn Fields, Holborn, London, WC2.

Lyceum Theatre (exterior): Trinity House, Trinity Square, Tower Hill, London EC3.

Lyceum Theatre (auditorium sequences): Aldwych Theatre, Aldwych, London, WC2.

Guy's Hospital (exterior): Somerset House, Strand, London, WC2.

Royal Mews (exterior): Osterley Park House, Isleworth, Middlesex, TW7 4RB.

King Charles Street in Westminster, which runs between the Foreign Office and the Treasury, one block away from Downing Street, is the huge Victorian street seen during the opening credits and throughout the film. It does however have restricted access to the public, because many important Parliamentarians work there.

Doubling as the exterior of Scotland Yard is Lincoln's Inn, which can be found in Holborn, London.

Jack the Ripper: Doubling as Scotland Yard is Lincoln's Inn, Lincoln's Inn Fields, Holborn, London. (Photograph by the author.)

Trinity House in Trinity Square, London, built in 1796, doubles as the exterior of the Lyceum Theatre. The interior, where actor Richard Mansfield (Armand Assante) gives his performance as Jekyll and Hyde, was filmed in the auditorium of the West End Alwdych Theatre, built in 1905.

The courtyard of the highly impressive Somerset House, off the Strand, doubles as the exterior of Guy's Hospital (see the chapter "Locations — In Detail" for a more in-depth look). The courtyard of Osterley Park House in Isleworth doubles as the Royal Mews, where Frederick Abberline (Michael Caine) and George Godley (Lewis Collins) meet up with John Netley (George Sweeney)—the Ripper's accomplice.

As a note of interest, the courtyard at Osterley Park House does look remarkably like the real Mews at Buckingham Palace.

"When we filmed on King Charles Street for the opening credits, we used over 80 horses and 46 horse-drawn vehicles — a record, I believe. They came from all over Britain, and completely filled the nearby space of Horse Guards

***Jack the Ripper*:** Featuring as the exterior of the Lyceum Theatre is Trinity House, Trinity Square, Tower Hill, London. (Photograph by the author.)

parade where the queen's birthday parades are held. Members of Parliament actually came out of their offices with their staff to watch us filming, and to find out how much it had cost me."— producer-director-co-writer David Wickes

Jekyll & Hyde
David Wickes Productions (1989)

Cast: Michael Caine, Cheryl Ladd, Joss Ackland, Ronald Pickup, Diane Keen, Kim Thomson, David Schofield, Lee Montague, Miriam Karlin, Lionel Jeffries

Screenplay-Producer-Director: David Wickes

Robert Louis Stevenson's all-time classic, telling the infamous story of a bold experiment which goes tragically wrong, turning Dr. Jekyll into the hideous and murderous Mr. Hyde.

Locations: London Street (opening credits): Somerset House, Strand, London, WC2.

Theatre: Richmond Theatre, The Green, Richmond, Surrey, TW9 1QJ.

The London street seen during the opening credits and throughout the film is actually the courtyard of Somerset House in London.

Doubling as the theatre, where Dr. Jekyll (Michael Caine) and his wife (Cheryl Ladd) see an opera performance, is Richmond Theatre in Richmond, Surrey.

Killer's Moon
Rothernorth Films (1978)

Cast: Anthony Forrest, Nigel Gregory, Tom Marshall, Georgina Kean, David Jackson, Jane Hayden, Hilda Braid, Hugh Ross, Chubby Oates

Producers: Alan Birkinshaw, Gordon Keymer

Screenplay-Director: Alan Birkinshaw

Jack the Ripper: Featuring as the exterior of Guy's Hospital is Somerset House, Strand, London. (Photograph by the author.)

A coachload of schoolgirls stranded in a derelict hotel are terrorized by four escaped lunatics.

Location: The Hotel (exterior and interior): Armathwaite Hall Hotel, Bassenthwaite, Keswick, Cumbria, CA12 4RE.

Rich in history, the Armathwaite Hall Hotel goes back to the 1300s when it was built as a house for Benedictine nuns, before becoming a stately home, and then finally a hotel in the 1930s. It is surrounded by the beautifully scenic Lake District, and within the secluded splendor of 400 acres of deer park and woodland.

The Lair of the White Worm
White Lair (1988)

Cast: Amanda Donohue, Hugh Grant, Catherine Oxenberg, Peter Capaldi, Sammi Davis, Stratford Johns

Screenplay-Producer-Director: Ken Russell

A female vampire attempts to make human sacrifices to an ancient snake god.

Locations: D'Ampton Hall (exterior and interior): Knebworth House, Knebworth, Hertfordshire, SG3 6PY.

Temple House (exterior and interior): Gaddesden Place, Great Gaddesden, Hemel Hempstead, Hertfordshire, HP2 6EX.

Doubling as the home of Lord James D'Ampton (Hugh Grant) is Knebworth House (see the chapter "Locations—In Detail"). Gaddesden Place features as Temple House, the home of Lady Sylvia Marsh (Amanda Donohoe), who is not quite what she seems.

The Legacy
Pethurst Ltd (1978)

Cast: Katharine Ross, Sam Elliott, Ian Hogg, John Standing, Margaret Tyzack, Charles Gray, Lee Montague, Roger Daltrey, Hildegard Neil, Patsy Smart
Screenplay: Jimmy Sangster, Patrick Tilley, Paul Wheeler
Producer: David Foster
Director: Richard Marquand

All the guests at a country house have been lured there in order to determine which one is to inherit a satanic legacy.

Location: Mountolive's Manor House (exterior and interior): Loseley Park House, Loseley Park, Guildford, Surrey, GU3 1HS.

See the chapter "Locations — In Detail" for a more in-depth look at Loseley Park House, which features throughout *The Legacy* as the country home of Jason Mountolive (John Standing) and his guests (Katharine Ross, Sam Elliott, Charles Gray, Roger Daltrey, etc.).

The Legend of Hell House
20th Century–Fox (1973)

Cast: Pamela Franklin, Roddy McDowall, Clive Revill, Gayle Hunnicutt, Roland Culver, Peter Bowles, Michael Gough
Screenplay: Richard Matheson
Producers: Albert Fennell, Norman T. Herman
Director: John Hough

***The Legend of Hell House*:** One of the griffins at Wykehurst Place, Bolney, West Sussex, which featured as part of "Hell House." Courtesy of Simon Flynn.

A scientist, his wife and two mediums are hired by a millionaire who is obsessed with knowing whether there is life beyond the grave. They are sent to investigate a haunted house, where previous hauntings have often led to the death of the psychics who attempted to probe its secret.

Studio: Elstree Studios, Borehamwood, Hertfordshire.

Location: The Meeting With Mr. Deutsch (interior and exterior): Blenheim Palace, Woodstock, Oxfordshire, OX20 1PX.

Hell House (exterior): Wykehurst Place, Wykehurst Park, Bolney, West Sussex.

This is the granddaddy of haunted house pictures. Doubling as Hell House is the star of the film, Wykehurst Place, a bizarre and rather haunting-looking mansion house, with sinister features like no other stately home in the country (see the chapter "Wykehurst Place" for a more in-depth look). It is here that Pamela Franklin, Roddy McDowall, Clive Revill, and Gayle Hunnicutt are subjected to the most terrifying night of their lives, at the hands of evil specter Emeric Belasco (Michael Gough).

The pre-credit sequence in which Dr. Barrett (Revill) meets up with Mr. Deutsch (Roland Culver) was shot on location at Blenheim Palace in Oxfordshire, and makes full use of both the interior and exterior.

"I wanted the audience to have no doubt in their minds that the house we used for filming, which turned out to be the perfect Wykehurst Place, was haunted." — director John Hough

Legend of the Werewolf
Tyburn Productions (1974)

Cast: Peter Cushing, David Rintoul, Ron Moody, Hugh Griffith, Roy Castle, Lynn Dalby, Stefan Gryff, Renee Houston, Marjorie Yates, Norman Mitchell, Patrick Holt, John Harvey, David Bailie, Michael Ripper
Screenplay: John Elder
Producer: Kevin Francis
Director: Freddie Francis

A young man working at a Paris zoo discovers that he changes into a werewolf when the moon is full.

Studio: Pinewood Studios, Buckinghamshire.
Location: Woodland: Black Park, Black Park Road, Wexham, Buckinghamshire, SL3 6DR.

The opening credits sequence, shot as if looking through the eyes of a wolf, was filmed at Black Park.

The Living Dead at the Manchester Morgue
Hallmark Releasing Corporation (1974)

Cast: Ray Lovelock, Christine Galbo, Arthur Kennedy, Aldo Massasso, Giorgio Trestini, Roberto Posse, Isabel Mestre
Screenplay: Sandro Continenza, Marcello Coscia
Producer: Edmundo Amati
Director: Jorge Grau

An ultrasonic pest control device brings the dead back to life in a small village.

The Living Dead at the Manchester Morgue: Doubling as the isolated and creepy cemetery is St. Michael and All Angels Church, School Lane, Hathersage, Derbyshire.

The Living Dead at the Manchester Morgue: St. Michael and All Angels Church, School Lane, Hathersage, Derbyshire, where George and Edna are confronted by several bloodthirsty zombies, and try to escape through the door (pictured) at the back of the church. (Photograph by the author.)

Locations: Stream with Stepping Stones: Thorpe Cloud, Dovedale, Nr. Ashbourne, Derbyshire.

The Cemetery: St. Michael and All Angels Church, School Lane, Hathersage, Derbyshire, S32 1BB.

Southgate Village: Market Place, Castleton, Derbyshire.

Southgate Hospital (exterior): Barnes Hospital, Kingsway, Cheadle, Cheshire, SK8 2NY.

Thorpe Cloud in Derbyshire, a very popular place for walkers, features in the scene in which Edna (Christine Galbo) is attacked in her car by a vicious zombie. When she tries to escape on foot, she falls in the stream next to the stepping stones.

The creepy cemetery is St. Michael and All Angels Church, where George (Ray Lovelock) and Edna are confronted by several bloodthirsty zombies, and try to escape through a door at the back of the church, which leads to a small room.

St. Michael and All Angels is the burial place of Little John (of Robin Hood fame).

Castleton, in the Peak District of Derbyshire, which is surrounded by spectacular scenery, doubles as Southgate Village. Barnes Hospital, built in the late 1800s, features throughout the film, and notably in the climax, when it is overrun by zombies. Barnes closed its doors as a hospital in 1999, and is presently derelict, but being considered for luxurious apartments.

Long Time Dead
Canal+ (2002)

Cast: Joe Absolom, Lara Belmont, Melanie Gutteridge, Lukas Haas, James Hillier, Alec Newman, Tom Bell
Screenplay: Eitan Arrusi, Chris Baker, Daniel Bronzite, Andy Day
Producer: James Gay-Rees
Director: Marcus Adams

A group of students dare each other to try out a Ouija board, and what starts out as harmless fun rapidly turns into a nightmare.

Location: The Students House (exterior): St. Augustine's Vicarage, Lynton Road, Bermondsey, London, SE1.

The rather creepy-looking St. Augustine's Vicarage doubles as the lodging house of a group of students.

Lust for a Vampire
Hammer Films (1970)

Cast: Ralph Bates, Michael Johnson, Barbara Jefford, Suzanna Leigh, Yutte Stensgaard, Mike Raven, Helen Christie, Pippa Steel, Harvey Hall, Christopher Neame, Eric Chitty
Screenplay: Tudor Gates
Producers: Harry Fine, Michael Style
Director: Jimmy Sangster

In 1830, an English writer discerns that a pupil in an exclusive mid-European girls' school is a reincarnated vampire.

Studio: Elstree Studios, Borehamwood, Hertfordshire.

Lust for a Vampire: On location at Hunton Park, Essex Lane, Kings Langley, Hertfordshire. Courtesy of Terry Pearce.

Lust for a Vampire: Doubling as the mid–European girls' school is Hunton Park, Essex Lane, Kings Langley, Hertfordshire. Courtesy of Ruth Potter.

Locations: The School (exterior and interior): Hunton Park, Essex Lane, Kings Langley, Hertfordshire, WD4 8PN.

Hunton Park, originally called Hazelwood House, is a charming Queen Anne private home. It has recently been re-developed to become part of a chain of training and conference venues.

Madhouse
Amicus Films (1973)

Cast: Vincent Price, Peter Cushing, Robert Quarry, Adrienne Corri, Natasha Pyne, Linda Hayden, Barry Dennen, Michael Parkinson
Screenplay: Greg Morrison
Producer: Milton Subotsky
Director: Jim Clark

A famous horror film star comes out of retirement, only to be implicated in a series of grisly murders.

Location: Madhouse (exterior): Pyrford Place, Warren Lane, Pyrford, West Byfleet, Surrey, GU22.

Madhouse: In the grounds of Pyrford Place was built a more modern-looking house. However, the gates and gardens remain exactly the same. Courtesy of Simon Flynn.

Rainbow Television (interior and exterior): London Television Centre, Upper Ground, London, SE1 9LT.

Pyrford Place, a fifteenth century manor house which doubled as the home of Herbert Flay (Peter Cushing), was demolished in the early 1990s, and in its place was built a more modern house (still named Pyrford Place) with luxurious apartments. However, the garden and gates to the house remain the same as when the film was shot there.

Doubling as Rainbow Television in the film where Paul Toombes (Vincent Price) is stalked by a murderous masked assailant is London Television Centre (previously London Weekend Television).

The Masks of Death
Tyburn Productions (1984)

Cast: Peter Cushing, John Mills, Anne Baxter, Ray Milland, Anton Diffring, Gordon Jackson, Susan Penhaligon, Marcus Gilbert, Jenny Laird, James Cossins

Screenplay: N. J. Crisp

Producer: Norman Priggen
Director: Roy Ward Baker

Sherlock Holmes ventures out of retirement to solve one last mysterious case.

Location: Von Felseck's House (exterior): St. Huberts, St. Huberts Lane, Gerrards Cross, Buckinghamshire.

Doubling as the home of Von Felseck (Anton Diffring) is St. Huberts, where Sherlock Holmes (Peter Cushing) and Doc Watson (John Mills) uncover a deadly plot.

The Monster Club
Amicus Films (1980)

Cast: Vincent Price, John Carradine, Barbara Kellerman, Simon Ward, Donald Pleasence, Richard Johnson, Britt Ekland, Stuart Whitman, Lesley Dunlop, Patrick Magee, Geoffrey Bayldon, James Laurenson
Screenplay: Edward Abraham, Valerie Abraham
Producer: Milton Subotsky
Director: Roy Ward Baker

A vampire takes his victim to a club, at which assorted monsters tell their stories.

Studio: Elstree Studios, Borehamwood, Hertfordshire.
Location: Raven's House (exterior and interior): Knebworth House, Knebworth, Hertfordshire, SG3 6PY.

See the chapter "Locations — In Detail" for a more in-depth look at Knebworth House, which features here in the segment "Shadmock" as the stately home of, Raven, a man with a sinister secret.

Mother Riley Meets the Vampire
Renown (1952)

Cast: Arthur Lucan, Bela Lugosi, Dora Bryan, Richard Wattis, Hattie Jacques, Dandy Nichols, Charles Lloyd Pack
Screenplay: Val Valentine
Producer-Director: John Gilling

A vampire-like madman plans to control the world with the help of his robot, which accidentally gets shipped to an old washer woman, Mother Riley.

Studio: Nettlefold Studios, Hurst Grove, Walton-on-Thames, Surrey.

Horror legend Bela Lugosi filmed in England on three separate occasions, the last time being when he appeared in this comic horror. All his scenes were shot inside Nettlefold Studio, which was mostly demolished in the early 1960s (see the chapter "The Studios" for a more in-depth look).

The Mummy
Hammer Films (1959)

Cast: Peter Cushing, Christopher Lee, Yvonne Furneaux, Eddie Byrne, Felix Aylmer, Raymond Huntley, George Pastell, Michael Ripper, George Woodbridge, Harold Goodwin, Denis Shaw, Gerald Lawson, Willoughby Gray
Screenplay: Jimmy Sangster
Producer: Michael Carreras
Director: Terence Fisher

An Egyptian mummy brought to England by archaeologists is awoken by the reading of a sacred scroll, and begins killing those who disturbed its tomb.

Studio: Bray Studios, Windsor, Berkshire.
Location: John Banning's home (exterior): Down Place, Bray Film Studios, Water Oakley, Windsor, SL4 5UG.

Built by the River Thames as a private house, Down Place would go on to become the home of Bray Studios in the late 1940s, and features here as the

The Mummy: Doubling as the home of John Banning (Peter Cushing) is Down Place, Bray Film Studios, Water Oakley, Windsor. Courtesy of Wayne Kinsey.

home of John Banning (Peter Cushing), who becomes the target of Kharis the Mummy (Christopher Lee).

The Mummy Returns
Universal Pictures (2001)

Cast: Brendan Fraser, Rachel Weisz, John Hannah, Arnold Vosloo, The Rock, Alun Armstrong, Freddie Boath
Producers: Sean Daniel, James Jacks
Screenplay-Director: Stephen Sommers

The mummified body of an Egyptian high priest, Imhotep, is shipped to the British Museum in London, where he wakes and begins his campaign of terror.

Studio: Pinewood Studios, Buckinghamshire.
Location: The British Museum (exterior): University College, Gower Street, London, WC1E 6BT.

Doubling as the British Museum is University College, which also features as the same building in the mummy film *The Awakening*.

The Mutations
Cyclone (1974)

Cast: Donald Pleasence, Tom Baker, Brad Harris, Julie Ege, Michael Dunn, Scott Antony, Jill Haworth, Lisa Collings
Screenplay: Robert D. Weinbach, Edward Mann
Producer: Robert D. Weinbach
Director: Jack Cardiff

A scientist experiments in cross-breeding people with plants.

Location: Dr. Nolter's House (exterior and interior): Oakley Court Hotel, Windsor Road, Water Oakley, Windsor, SL4 5UR.

Dr. Nolter (Donald Pleasence) and his mutant sidekick (Tom Baker) are up to some gruesome business behind closed doors; their home happens to be the one and only Oakley Court, a horror movie favorite.

The Mystery of the Mary Celeste
Hammer Films (1935)

Cast: Bela Lugosi, Shirley Grey, Arthur Margetson, Edmund Willard, Dennis Hoey

Producer: C.M. Woolf
Screenplay-Director: Denison Clift

A mad sailor kills his fellow crew members and then throws himself overboard.

Studio: Nettlefold Studios, Hurst Grove, Walton-on-Thames, Surrey.

Legendary horror star Bela Lugosi made his first appearance in a British movie in this low-budget horror made in the early days of Hammer.

The Nanny
Hammer Films (1965)

Cast: Bette Davis, Wendy Craig, Jill Bennett, James Villiers, William Dix, Pamela Franklin, Maurice Denham, Jack Watling
Screenplay-Producer: Jimmy Sangster
Director: Seth Holt

The Nanny: Doubling as the Fanes' (Wendy Craig and James Villiers) apartment is 30 Chester Terrace, Regent's Park, London. (Photograph by the author.)

A young boy discovers his nanny's guilty secret, and has to devise a means of thwarting her efforts to silence him.

Studio: Elstree Studios, Borehamwood, Hertfordshire.
Location: The Fanes' Apartment (exterior): 30 Chester Terrace, Regent's Park, London, NW1.
Master Joey's School (exterior): Wall Hall Mansion, Church Lane, Aldenham, Watford, Hertfordshire, WD2 8AT.

30 Chester Terrace appears at the opening of the movie as the home of the Fanes (Wendy Craig and James Villiers). The mansion house Wall Hall in Hertfordshire doubles as Master Joey's school. This impressive looking 18th century manor is presently being turned into luxury apartments. It is surrounded by a ghastly housing development which will totally ruin the mansion's grounds.

The Night Digger
Metro-Goldwyn-Mayer (1971)

Cast: Patricia Neal, Nicholas Clay, Pamela Browne, Jean Anderson, Yootha Joyce, Peter Sallis, Graham Crowden, Brigit Forsyth
Screenplay: Roald Dahl
Producers: Alan D. Courtney, Norman S. Powell
Director: Alastair Reid

A frustrated spinster protects a handyman who is clearly guilty of murder.

Studio: Twickenham Studios, Middlesex.
Location: The Towers (exterior and interior): Oakley Court Hotel, Windsor Road, Water Oakley, Windsor, SL4 5UR.

Seen as the Gothic home of Maura Prince (Patricia Neal) and her mother (Pamela Browne) is Oakley Court. You can read more about this in the chapter "Locations — In Detail."

Night of the Big Heat
Planet Film Productions (1967)

Cast: Christopher Lee, Peter Cushing, Patrick Allen, Sarah Lawson, Jane Merrow, William Lucas, Kenneth Cope, Jack Bligh, Sydney Bromley, Percy Herbert
Screenplay: Ronald Liles
Producer: Tom Blakeley
Director: Terence Fisher

Invaders from outer space take over a remote Scottish island, causing a heatwave and several human deaths.

Studio: Pinewood Studios, Buckinghamshire.
Location: The Swan (exterior): The Swan Inn, Broughton Road, Milton Keynes Village, Milton Keynes, Buckinghamshire, MK10 9AH.

The Swan Inn, a seventeenth century, allegedly haunted country pub in Buckinghamshire, doubles as, yes you've guessed it, The Swan, where Peter Cushing, Christopher Lee, Patrick Allen, Sarah Lawson, Jane Merrow, and Kenneth Cope sweat it out in an inexplicable winter heat wave, while drinking the contents of the bar.

Night of the Demon
Sabre Film Production (1957)

Cast: Dana Andrews, Peggy Cummins, Niall MacGinnis, Brian Wilde, Maurice Denham, Liam Redmond, Reginald Beckwith
Producer: Frank Bevis
Director: Jacques Tourneur

An occultist dispatches his enemies by raising a giant medieval devil.

Studio: Elstree Studios, Borehamwood, Hertfordshire.
Location: Lufford Hall (exterior): Brocket Hall, Welwyn, Hertfordshire, AL8 7XG.
Railway Line: Bricket Wood Station, Station Road, Bricket Wood, Hertfordshire, AL2.

Night of the Demon: The climax of the film in which Karswell (Niall MacGinnis) is dispatched on the railway line by the very demon he summoned was filmed at Bricket Wood Station, Station Road, Bricket Wood, Hertfordshire. (Photograph by the author.)

Doubling as the house of the evil Julian Karswell (Niall MacGinnis) is Brocket Hall, which you can read more about in the chapter "Locations — In Detail."

The end sequence on the Railway Line, where Karswell is slain by the demon he summoned, was filmed on the line at Bricket Wood station. The station has changed quite considerably since 1957 and one track has been removed, leaving just one line.

The Nightcomers
Scimitar Productions (1971)

Cast: Marlon Brando, Stephanie Beacham, Thora Hird, Harry Andrews, Verna Harvey, Christopher Ellis, Anna Palk
Screenplay: Michael Hastings
Producer-Director: Michael Winner

Aberrant sexual activities between the gardener and housekeeper of a stately home are witnessed by a young boy and girl who then do acts of evil.

Location: Bly House (exterior and interior): Sawston Hall, Sawston, Cambridge, CB2 4JR.

Sawston Hall, a Tudor manor house built in the sixteenth century, doubles as Bly House, where Stephanie Beacham and Marlon Brando get up to some rather naughty business.

Nothing but the Night
Charlemagne Productions (1972)

Cast: Christopher Lee, Peter Cushing, Diana Dors, Georgia Brown, Keith Barron, Fulton Mackay, Gwyneth Strong, Michael Gambon, Shelagh Fraser, Duncan Lamont, Kathleen Byron
Screenplay: Brian Hayles
Producer: Anthony Nelson Keys
Director: Peter Sasdy

Nothing but the Night: Doubling as "Inver House," the orphanage for demonic children, is Stanmore Hall, Wood Lane, Stanmore, Middlesex. (Photograph by the author.)

94 *The Old Dark House*

Children at an orphanage are possessed by demonic forces after being injected with the life essences of dead trustees.

Studio: Pinewood Studios, Buckinghamshire.
Location: Inver House (exterior): Stanmore Hall, Wood Lane, Stanmore, Middlesex, HA7.

Doubling as Inver House, the orphanage for demonic children, is the very grand and quite beautiful Stanmore Hall.

The Old Dark House
Hammer Films (1962)

Cast: Tom Poston, Janette Scott, Robert Morley, Joyce Grenfell, Mervyn Johns, Fenella Fielding, Peter Bull
Screenplay: Robert Dillon
Producer-Director: William Castle

An American accepts an invitation to visit Femm Hall, and finds the inhabitants either mad or homicidal.

Location: Femm Hall (exterior): Oakley Court Hotel, Windsor Road, Water Oakley, Windsor, SL4 5UR.

Oakley Court features as Femm Hall, a house with some rather sinister occupants.

The Omen
20th Century–Fox (1976)

Cast: Gregory Peck, Lee Remick, Billie Whitelaw, David Warner, Patrick Troughton, Leo McKern, Harvey Stephens, Martin Benson, Holly Palance, John Stride, Tommy Duggan
Screenplay: David Seltzer
Producer: Harvey Bernhard
Director: Richard Donner

The adopted child of an ambassador to Great Britain shows unnerving signs of being the Anti-Christ.

Studio: Shepperton Studios, Middlesex.
Locations: Ambassador Thorn's Home (exterior and interior): Pyrford Court, Pyrford Common Road, Pyrford, West Byfleet, Surrey, GU22.
Father Brennan's Church (exterior): All Saints Church, Steeple Close, Fulham, London, SW6.

The Omen: Pyrford Court, Pyrford Common Road, Pyrford, West Byfleet, Surrey, features throughout the film as the home of Ambassador Thorn (Gregory Peck). Courtesy of Simon Flynn.

Doubling as the home of Ambassador Thorn (Gregory Peck), his wife (Lee Remick), and their loving son Damien (Harvey Stephens) is Pyrford Court in Surrey. Situated on the bank of the River Thames, All Saints Church is the location where Father Brennan (Patrick Troughton) is fatally impaled.

Omen III — The Final Conflict
20th Century–Fox (1981)

Cast: Sam Neill, Rossano Brazzi, Don Gordon, Lisa Harrow, Mason Adams, Robert Arden, Norman Bird, Tommy Duggan
Screenplay: Andrew Birkin
Producer: Harvey Bernhard
Director: Graham Baker

The Anti-Christ, Damien Thorn, has a final showdown with Christ.

Studio: Elstree Studios, Borehamwood, Hertfordshire.
Locations: Damien Thorn's Residence (exterior and interior): Brocket Hall, Welwyn, Hertfordshire, AL8 7XG.

Above, left: The Omen: Doubling as the church where Father Brennan (Patrick Troughton) is fatally impaled is All Saints Church, Steeple Close, Fulham, London. (Photograph by the author.) *Above, right: Omen III—The Final Conflict:* The murder of Brother Matteus, mistaken for Damien Thorn, was filmed at the derelict Hermit's Chapel, Roche Rock, Roche, Cornwall. (Photograph by the author.)

Observatory Sequences (interior): University of London Observatory, 553 Watford Way, Mill Hill Park, London, NW7 2QS.

Chapel Ruins—The Murder of Brother Matteus: The Hermit's Chapel (Derelict), Roche Rock, Roche, Cornwall.

Careening Baby Carriage Site: Lansdowne Rise, Notting Hill, London, W11.

Damien's Death Site: Fountains Abbey, Ripon, North Yorkshire, HG4 3DY.

The dwelling place of Damien Thorn the Anti-Christ (Sam Neill) is Brocket Hall, using both the interior and exterior.

Seen in several scenes throughout the movie is the University of London Observatory. Tours of this building are conducted for a limited period throughout the year.

The sequence in which Brother Matteus (Tommy Duggan) is stabbed to death by members of his brethren who have mistaken him for Damien Thorn, was shot at the derelict, and almost unreal-looking Hermit's Chapel in Cornwall (apparently haunted), which was built by a hermit in 1409. Still today it looks out over a vast Cornish moorland.

Lansdowne Rise in London's Notting Hill was the location for the terrifying sequence in which a baby carriage careens down a hill into a busy road full of traffic.

The end of the movie (the death of Damien) was filmed at Fountains Abbey in Yorkshire. Read more about this historic site in the chapter "Locations—In Detail."

Peeping Tom
Anglo-Amalgamated Productions (1960)

Cast: Carl Boehm, Moira Shearer, Anna Massey, Maxine Audley, Brenda Bruce, Esmond Knight, Michael Goodliffe, Jack Watson, Shirley Ann Field, Miles Malleson
Screenplay: Leo Marks
Producer-Director: Michael Powell

Peeping Tom: The opening murder sequence was filmed at Newman Arms, 23 Rathbone Street, London. (Photograph by the author.)

98 *Persecution*

***Peeping Tom*:** Featuring as the newsagents shop where dirty old man Miles Malleson buys pornographic photographs is the "Caffe," 29 Rathbone Place, London. (Photograph by the author.)

> *A demented cine photographer is fascinated by the idea of murdering women on film, and capturing the look of fear on their faces.*

Studio: Pinewood Studios, Buckinghamshire.
Location: Opening Murder Site: Newman Arms, 23 Rathbone Street, London, W1T 1NQ.
The Newsagents Shop (exterior): Caffe, 29 Rathbone Place, London, W1.

The opening sequence where Carl Boehm murders prostitute Brenda Bruce was shot at the Newman Arms, and in the passageway next to it.

29 Rathbone Place, which is now a café, doubled as The Newsagent Shop, where dirty old man Miles Malleson buys pornographic photographs.

Persecution
Tyburn Productions (1974)

Cast: Lana Turner, Ralph Bates, Trevor Howard, Suzan Farmer, Ronald Howard, Patrick Allen, Shelagh Fraser

Screenplay: Robert Hutton, Rosemary Wootten
Producer: Kevin Francis
Director: Don Chaffey

A rich, crippled American woman living in England dominates her son, who hates and fears her.

Location: The Masters House (exterior): Denham Place, Denham Village, Denham, Buckinghamshire.

Doubling as the home of Carrie Masters (Lana Turner) is the large private house Denham Place in Denham Village. This vast property has a ten-foot stone wall surrounding it. Buckingham Palace might be easier to gain entrance to.

The Phantom of the Opera
Hammer Films (1962)

Cast: Herbert Lom, Heather Sears, Thorley Walters, Edward De Souza, Michael Gough, John Harvey, Miriam Karlin, Miles Malleson, Patrick Troughton, Michael Ripper, Harold Goodwin, Marne Maitland
Screenplay: John Elder
Producer: Anthony Hinds
Director: Terence Fisher

A hideously disfigured composer takes refuge in the sewers below the Paris Opera House. Falling in love with a girl's voice, he abducts her to sing in his opera.

Studio: Bray Studios, Windsor, Berkshire.
Location: Paris Opera House (auditorium sequences): Wimbledon Theatre, The Broadway, Wimbledon, London, SW19 1QG.

Doubling as the interior of the Paris Opera House is Wimbledon Theatre with its Victorian auditorium.

The Plague of the Zombies
Hammer Films (1965)

Cast: Andre Morell, Diane Clare, Jacqueline Pearce, John Carson, Brook Williams, Michael Ripper, Alex Davion, Marcus Hammond, Dennis Chinnery
Screenplay: Peter Bryan
Producer: Anthony Nelson Keys
Director: John Gilling

A voodoo-practicing Cornish squire raises men from the dead as zombies and uses them to work in his tin mine.

Studio: Bray Studios, Windsor, Berkshire.
Location: Woodland Sequences: Black Park, Black Park Road, Wexham, Buckinghamshire, SL3 6DR.

Black Park features throughout the film. The exterior of the tin mine was constructed there.

Prey
Supreme Films (1977)

Cast: Glory Annen, Sally Faulkner, Barry Stokes, Sandy Chinney, Eddie Stacey, Jerry Crampton
Screenplay: Max Cuff
Producers: Terence Marcel, David Wimbury
Director: Norman J. Warren

An alien who likes to eat the flesh of humans takes over the body of a young man and is invited to stay the night by two lesbians, one of whom is a murderer.

Location: Jessica's House (exterior and interior): Littleton Park House, Shepperton Studios, Studios Road, Shepperton, Middlesex, TW17 0QD.

Doubling as the home of Jessica (Glory Annen) is Littleton Park House at Shepperton Studios.

The Quatermass Xperiment
Hammer Films (1955)

Cast: Brian Donlevy, Jack Warner, Richard Wordsworth, Thora Hird, Gordon Jackson, Harold Lang, Lionel Jeffries, Sam Kydd, Jane Asher, Marianne Stone
Screenplay: Richard Landau, Val Guest
Producer: Anthony Hinds
Director: Val Guest

When a rocketship returns from space, two of its three crew members have disappeared and the third is slowly being taken over by an extraterrestrial fungus.

Studio: Bray Studios, Windsor, Berkshire.
Locations: Oakley Green Village: Bray, Nr. Windsor, Berkshire.

Westminster Abbey (exterior): Westminster Abbey, Westminster, London, SW1P 3PA.

Oakley Green Village, where the spaceship crashlands at the opening of the film, is actually Bray in Windsor, just down the road from Bray Studios.

Westminster Abbey (see the chapter "Locations — In Detail" for a more in-depth look), an architectural masterpiece, features at the climax when the alien creature takes refuge there, and Prof. Quatermass (Brian Donlevy) and the army have to think of a way to destroy it.

Quatermass 2
Hammer Films (1957)

Cast: Brian Donlevy, John Longden, Sidney James, Bryan Forbes, William Franklyn, Charles Lloyd Pack, Percy Herbert, Michael Ripper
Screenplay: Nigel Kneale, Val Guest
Producer: Anthony Hinds
Director: Val Guest

A research plant operating under military secrecy is supposed to be making synthetic foods, but is in fact an acclimatization center for invaders from outer space.

Studio: New Elstree Studios, Elstree, Hertfordshire.
Location: Research Plant (exterior): Shell Haven Oil Refinery, Stanford-le-Hope, Essex, SS17 9LD.

The huge Shell Haven Oil Refinery in Essex doubles as a rather sinister research plant where alien activity is taking place.

Repulsion
Compton Films (1965)

Cast: Catherine Deneuve, Ian Hendry, John Fraser, Patrick Wymark, Yvonne Furneaux, Renee Houston, James Villiers, Mike Pratt
Screenplay: Roman Polanski, Gerard Brach
Producer: Gene Gutowski
Director: Roman Polanski

A withdrawn young woman slowly descends into madness when left alone in her gloomy flat for a few days while her sister goes on holiday.

Studio: Twickenham Studios, Middlesex.
Location: Carol's Flat (exterior and interior): Kensington Mansions, Trebovir Road, Kensington, London, SW5.

Featured as Carol's (Catherine Deneuve) gloomy flat is the not so gloomy — actually, quite ordinary — Kensington Mansions.

The Rocky Horror Picture Show
20th Century–Fox (1975)

Cast: Tim Curry, Susan Sarandon, Barry Bostwick, Richard O'Brien, Meatloaf, Charles Gray, Patricia Quinn, Koo Stark, Christopher Biggins
Screenplay: Richard O'Brien, Jim Sharman
Producer: Michael White
Director: Jim Sharman

A straight couple take refuge in a house full of weirdos, where sex, transvestism and rock music are all the rage.

Studio: Bray Studios, Windsor, Berkshire.

Repulsion: Featuring as the gloomy flat of Carol (Catherine Deneuve) is Kensington Mansions, Trebovir Road, Kensington, London. (Photograph by the author.)

Location: The Frankenstein Place (exterior and interior): Oakley Court Hotel, Windsor Road, Water Oakley, Windsor, SL4 5UR.

Only one gothic mansion, Oakley Court, could play the home of Dr. Frank-N-Furter (Tim Curry), Riff Raff (Richard O'Brien) and Magenta (Patricia Quinn), in this cult classic.

The Satanic Rites of Dracula
Hammer Films (1972)

Cast: Christopher Lee, Peter Cushing, Michael Coles, William Franklyn, Freddie Jones, Joanna Lumley, Richard Vernon, Patrick Barr, Valerie Van Ost
Screenplay: Don Houghton
Producer: Roy Skeggs
Director: Alan Gibson

An outbreak of vampirism in London is traced to the presence of Count Dracula, who plans to unleash a deadly plague upon the world.

Studio: Elstree Studios, Borehamwood, Hertfordshire.

The Satanic Rites of Dracula: High Canons, Buckettsland Lane, Well End, Hertfordshire, doubles as "Pelham House," the hiding place of Count Dracula (Christopher Lee). (Photograph by the author.)

Location: Pelham House (exterior): High Canons, Buckettsland Lane, Well End, Hertfordshire, WD6 5PL.

The Keeley Foundation (exterior): Queen's Gate Lodge, 23a Elvaston Place, Kensington, London, SW7.

High Canons, a private house on a large country estate in Hertfordshire, doubles as Pelham House, the home and hiding place of Count Dracula (Christopher Lee) and his followers.

The Keeley Foundation where Freddie Jones is trying to create a new form of bubonic plague is Queen's Gate Lodge in Kensington.

Satan's Slave
Brent Walker (1976)

Cast: Michael Gough, Martin Potter, Candace Glendenning, Barbara Kellerman, James Bree, Celia Hewitt, Michael Craze

The Satanic Rites of Dracula: Doubling as "The Keeley Foundation," where Freddie Jones is trying to create a new form of bubonic plague, is Queen's Gate Lodge, 23a Elvaston Place, Kensington, London. (Photograph by the author.)

Screenplay: David McGillivray
Producers: Richard Crafter, Les Young
Director: Norman J. Warren

A young woman, caught up in a devil cult run by her uncle and cousin, is to become their next sacrifice.

Location: Alexander's House (exterior and interior): Admiral's Walk, Mill Lane, Pirbright, Nr. Woking, Surrey, GU24.

Admiral's Walk features as the home of Alexander (Michael Gough), the leader of a devil-worshipping cult.

Secret Ceremony
Universal Pictures (1969)

Cast: Elizabeth Taylor, Robert Mitchum, Mia Farrow, Pamela Brown, Peggy Ashcroft, Brook Williams
Screenplay: George Tabori
Producers: John Heyman, Norman Priggen

Secret Ceremony: The creepy mansion where Elizabeth Taylor plays disturbing mindgames with Mia Farrow is Debenham House, 8 Addison Road, Kensington, London. (Photograph by the author.)

Director: Joseph Losey

A prostitute mother and a young woman with a strange past.

Studio: Elstree Studios, Borehamwood, Hertfordshire.
Location: Mansion House (exterior): Debenham House, 8 Addison Road, Kensington, London, W14.

The creepy mansion where Elizabeth Taylor plays disturbing mindgames with Mia Farrow is Debenham House in Kensington, London.

Shaun of the Dead
Big Talk Productions (2004)

Cast: Simon Pegg, Kate Ashfield, Lucy Davis, Nick Frost, Dylan Moran, Bill Nighy, Penelope Wilton
Screenplay: Simon Pegg, Edgar Wright
Producer: Nira Park
Director: Edgar Wright

Shaun sets out to save his mum, his stepdad, his girlfriend and his friends from the dead, who are returning to life.

Studio: Ealing Studios, London.
Location: The Winchester Tavern (exterior): Duke of Albany, 39 Monson Road, New Cross, London, SE14 5EQ.

The Duke of Albany, now boarded up and derelict, doubles as The Winchester Tavern, where Shaun (Simon Pegg), Liz (Kate Ashfield), Ed (Nick Frost) and Barbara (Penelope Wilton) hide from the flesh-hungry undead walking the streets outside.

The Shining
Warner Bros. (1980)

Cast: Jack Nicholson, Shelley Duvall, Danny Lloyd, Scatman Crothers, Barry Nelson, Philip Stone, Barry Dennan

Shaun of the Dead: Doubling as the Winchester Tavern is the now boarded-up Duke of Albany, 39 Monson Road, New Cross, London. (Photograph by the author.)

Screenplay: Stanley Kubrick, Diane Johnson
Producer-Director: Stanley Kubrick

A man takes on the job of caretaker at a deserted hotel during its closed-down season. He slowly begins to fall victim to evil supernatural forces which make him undergo an unpleasant personality change. Soon he is threatening the lives of his wife and son.

Studio: Elstree Studios, Borehamwood, Hertfordshire.

The interior of the Overlook Hotel, where Shelley Duval finds herself hunted by axe-wielding husband Jack Nicholson, and the gigantic maze were actually sets on huge sound stages at Elstree Studios in Hertfordshire.

Scenes featuring the exterior of the hotel were shot on location at Colorado's Stanley Hotel. However a large replica of part of it was constructed on the back lot at Elstree.

Sleepy Hollow
Paramount Pictures (1999)

Cast: Johnny Depp, Christina Ricci, Miranda Richardson, Michael Gambon, Casper Van Dien, Jeffrey Jones, Richard Griffiths, Christopher Lee, Michael Gough, Ian McDiarmid, Christopher Walken, Alun Armstrong

Sleepy Hollow: Featuring briefly as a New York City street is the courtyard of Somerset House, Strand, London. (Photograph by the author.)

Screenplay: Andrew Kevin Walker
Producers: Scott Rudin, Adam Schroeder
Director: Tim Burton

A murderous Headless Horseman terrifies the little town of Sleepy Hollow.

Studio: Leavesden Film Studios, Hertfordshire.
Locations: New York City Street: Somerset House, Strand, London, WC2. Sleepy Hollow: Hambleden Estate, Nr. Marlow, Buckinghamshire.

At the beginning of the film, Ichabod Crane (Johnny Depp) is seen throwing a bird from the window of his home; the New York City Street you see outside is actually the courtyard of Somerset House in London.

The little town of Sleepy Hollow was actually an outdoor set constructed in a field on the Hambleden village estate in Buckinghamshire. Much of the rest of the film, including many of the forest sequences, were filmed on a huge sound stage at Leavesden Film Studios in Leavesden, Hertfordshire — home to the *Harry Potter* movies.

Son of Dracula
Cinemation Industries (1974)

Cast: Harry Nilsson, Ringo Starr, Dennis Price, Suzanna Leigh, Freddie Jones, Peter Frampton, Keith Moon, John Bonham, David Bailie, Dan Meaden, Skip Martin
Screenplay: Jennifer Jayne
Producers: Jerry Gross, Ringo Starr, Tim Van Rellim
Director: Freddie Francis

Due to be crowned King of the Netherworld by his mentor Merlin the Magician, Count Downe, the son of Count Dracula, falls in love with the beautiful but human Amber, and finds himself in conflict with Baron Frankenstein.

Locations: Castle Dracula (exterior): Wykehurst Place, Wykehurst Park, Bolney, West Sussex.

Merlin's House (exterior): London Business School, Regent's Park, London, NW1 4SA.

Son of Dracula: London Business School, Regent's Park, London, doubles as the home of Merlin (Ringo Starr). (Photograph by the author.)

No place could be better suited to play Castle Dracula than Wykehurst Place in Bolney. The London Business School in Regent's Park doubles as the home of Merlin (Ringo Starr).

The Sorcerers
Tigon Films (1967)

Cast: Boris Karloff, Catherine Lacey, Ian Ogilvy, Elizabeth Ercy, Susan George, Victor Henry, Dani Sheridan, Ivor Dean, Peter Fraser
Screenplay: Michael Reeves, Tom Baker, John Burke
Producers: Patrick Curtis, Tony Tenser
Director: Michael Reeves

An evil scientist and his wife devise a way of exercising control of other people's minds and hypnotize a young man to do their bidding.

Location: The Glory Hole Antique Shop (interior and exterior): 95 Lisson Grove, Marylebone, London.

Featured as Ian Ogilvy's antique shop The Glory Hole is 95 Lisson Grove, which is a real-life antique shop.

The Sorcerers: 95 Lisson Grove, Marylebone, London, features as The Glory Hole," the antique shop owned by Ian Ogilvy. (Photograph by the author.)

Straw Dogs
ABC Pictures Corporation (1971)

Cast: Dustin Hoffman, Susan George, Peter Vaughan, T.P. McKenna, David Warner, Colin Welland, Sally Thomsett, Peter Arne
Screenplay: David Zelag Goodman, Sam Peckinpah
Producer: Daniel Melnick
Director: Sam Peckinpah

An American academic and his wife settle in a Cornish village but find that the atmosphere is far from welcoming.

Studio: Twickenham Studios, Middlesex.
Locations: Wakeley Village: St. Buryan, Nr. Penzance, Cornwall.
Trencher's Cottage (exterior and

Top: Straw Dogs: Doubling as Wakeley Village is St. Buryan, Nr. Penzance, Cornwall. Courtesy of Brian Holland. *Bottom: Straw Dogs*: Doubling as the cottage where Dustin Hoffman and Susan George live is "Solomon's Island" Cottage, Tor Noon, Trevowhan, Nr. Morvah, Cornwall. Courtesy of Brian Holland.

interior): Solomon's Island Cottage, Tor Noon, Trevowhan, Nr. Morvah, Cornwall.

The small village of St. Buryan in Cornwall doubles as Wakeley Village in the film. The cottage where Dustin Hoffman and Susan George live is Solomon's Island, which stands all alone, totally unchanged, in the very isolated Tor Noon in Cornwall.

A Study in Terror
Compton Films (1965)

Cast: John Neville, Donald Houston, John Fraser, Anthony Quayle, Robert Morley, Cecil Parker, Barbara Windsor, Georgia Brown, Barry Jones, Adrienne Corri, Frank Finlay, Judi Dench
Screenplay: Donald Ford, Derek Ford
Producer: Henry E. Lester
Director: James Hill

Sherlock Holmes tracks down and uncovers the identity of Jack the Ripper in Victorian London.

Studio: Shepperton Studios, Middlesex.
Locations: The Duke of Shires Estate (exterior and interior): Osterley Park House, Isleworth, Middlesex, TW7 4RB.

Built in 1576, Osterley Park House features twice in the movie when Holmes (John Neville) and Watson (Donald Houston) visit the Duke of Shires (Barry Jones) and his son (John Fraser), who is not quite what he seems.

Tales from the Crypt
Amicus Films (1972)

Cast: Ralph Richardson, Peter Cushing, Joan Collins, Ian Hendry, Richard Greene, Robin Phillips, Nigel Patrick, Roy Dotrice, Patrick Magee, Geoffrey Bayldon, Barbara Murray, Chloe Franks, Angela Grant, David Markham, Robert Hutton
Screenplay-Producer: Milton Subotsky
Director: Freddie Francis

Five people exploring catacombs are confronted by a strange monk who predicts their nightmarish futures.

Studio: Shepperton Studios, Middlesex.
Locations: Graveyard (opening credits sequence): Highgate Cemetery, Swain's Lane, London, N6 6PJ.

Top: Tales from the Crypt: The apartment block where the lover of Ian Hendry lives in the segment "Reflection of Death" can be found on Wellington Close, Walton-on-Thames, Surrey. Courtesy of Simon Flynn. *Bottom: Tales from the Crypt*: "The Georgian Cottage," Queens Road, Hersham, Surrey, doubles as the posh home of the Elliotts (Robin Phillips and David Markham) in the segment "Poetic Justice." Courtesy of Simon Flynn.

Tales from the Crypt: Doubling as the home of Arthur Edward Grimsdyke (Peter Cushing) in the segment "Poetic Justice" is 122 Watersplash Road, Shepperton. Courtesy of Simon Flynn.*

Hillside in Segment "Reflection of Death" (exterior): Wellington Close, Walton-on-Thames, Surrey, KT12.

The Grimsdyke House in Segment "Poetic Justice" (exterior): 122 Watersplash Road, Shepperton, TW17.

The Elliott House in Segment "Poetic Justice" (exterior): The Georgian Cottage, Queens Road, Hersham, Surrey, KT12.

The Jason House in Segment "Wish You Were Here" (exterior): Pyrford Court, Pyrford Common Road, Pyrford, West Byfleet, Surrey GU22.

Elmridge Home for the Blind in Segment "Blind Alleys" (exterior): Brunel University, St. Margarets Road, Twickenham, TW1.

This, the fourth of the Amicus compendium pictures, and arguably their best, was the most successful at the box office—and here, thanks to the kindness of Terry Pearce (assistant director on the film), I am able to reveal for the very first time in print every important location from the movie.

The graveyard featured during the opening credits is the very creepy Highgate Cemetery. The apartment block (Hillside) where Susan (Angela Grant) lives in the segment "Reflection of Death" is actually on Wellington Close in Walton-on-Thames.

*"Sad to say, you cannot really connect this house any more with Peter Cushing's beloved old tramp."—Simon Flynn

In the segment "Poetic Justice," the home of Arthur Edward Grimsdyke (played beautifully by Peter Cushing, giving one of his finest performances) can actually be found at 122 Watersplash Road, Shepperton. The house has been altered quite considerably since 1971.

The posh home of the Elliotts (Robin Phillips and David Markham) in the same segment is 124 Queens Road in Hersham, Surrey.

Doubling as the home of the Jasons (Richard Greene and Barbara Murray) in the segment "Wish You Were Here" is Pyrford Court in Surrey.

The Elmridge Home for the Blind in the final segment "Blind Alleys," in which arrogant Nigel Patrick gets on the wrong side of a group of blind people, is Brunel University in Twickenham.

Directed by Freddie Francis, *Tales from the Crypt* is my favorite of all horror films, ranking Freddie as my favorite horror movie director. He had a rare talent for creating the right sort of chilling atmosphere.

Taste the Blood of Dracula
Hammer Films (1970)

Cast: Christopher Lee, Geoffrey Keen, Gwen Watford, Linda Hayden, Peter Sallis, Anthony Corlan, John Carson, Ralph Bates, Michael Ripper, Isla Blair, Martin Jarvis, Roy Kinnear
Screenplay: John Elder
Producer: Aida Young
Director: Peter Sasdy

A depraved peer involves three Victorian businessmen in the reanimation of Count Dracula.

Studio: Elstree Studios, Borehamwood, Hertfordshire.

Locations: Opening Pre-Credit Sequence Site: Scratchwood Nature Reserve, Elstree, Borehamwood, Hertfordshire.

Churchyard: St. Andrew's Church, Totteridge, London, N20 8PR.

Taste the Blood of Dracula: Scratchwood Nature Reserve, Elstree, Borehamwood, Hertfordshire, can be seen during the pre-credit sequence when Roy Kinnear stumbles across an impaled Count Dracula (Christopher Lee) in the forest. Courtesy of Ruth Potter.

Left: Taste the Blood of Dracula: St. Andrew's Church, Totteridge, London, doubles as the church where the three families congregate. Courtesy of Ruth Potter.
Right: Taste the Blood of Dracula: Doubling as the disused cemetery, the lair of Dracula (Christopher Lee), is Highgate Cemetery, Swain's Lane, London. Courtesy of Elmar Podlasly.

Disused Cemetery — The Lair of Dracula: Highgate Cemetery, Swain's Lane, London, N6 6PJ.

The pre-credit forest sequence where Roy Kinnear stumbles across an impaled Count Dracula (Christopher Lee) was filmed at Scratchwood Nature Reserve in Elstree, Hertfordshire. Scratchwood was used for a number of the later Hammer films as a substitute for Black Park.

Doubling as the church where the three families congregate is St. Andrew's Church in Totteridge. Highgate Cemetery features in the scene in which Count D. is resurrected by Lord Courtley (Ralph Bates), and then throughout the film as the hiding place of Dracula.

10 Rillington Place
Filmways Pictures (1970)

Cast: Richard Attenborough, Judy Geeson, John Hurt, Pat Heywood, Isobel Black, Robert Hardy, Andre Morrell, Sam Kydd, Rudolph Walker
Screenplay: Clive Exton

Producers: Leslie Linder, Martin Ransohoff
Director: Richard Fleischer

An account of the murderer John Christie, whose tenant Timothy Evans was hanged for his deeds.

Studio: Shepperton Studios, Middlesex.
Location: 10 Rillington Place (exterior): Ruston Mews, Notting Hill, London, W11.

This movie was filmed at the real Rillington Place, and some of the interiors were shot in the actual house where John Christie (played in the film by Lord Attenborough) committed several horrific murders. The street and house were demolished in the early 1970s, then rebuilt and renamed Ruston Mews. It is now only accessible to the street's residence.

"It was isolated and sometimes quite eerie filming at the real Rillington Place, because you couldn't quite dismiss what had happened there in the past."—Lord Attenborough

10 Rillington Place: Ruston Mews, Notting Hill, London, stands in the place of the now demolished Rillington Place, which was a location for the film. (Photograph by the author.)

Theatre of Blood
Cineman Productions (1973)

Cast: Vincent Price, Diana Rigg, Ian Hendry, Harry Andrews, Coral Browne, Jack Hawkins, Michael Hordern, Arthur Lowe, Robert Morley, Dennis Price, Milo O'Shea, Diana Dors, Robert Coote, Joan Hickson, Renee Asherson, Eric Sykes, Madeleine Smith
Screenplay: Anthony Greville-Bell
Producers: John Kohn, Stanley Mann
Director: Douglas Hickox

A mad ham classical theatre actor decides to take gruesome revenge on all the critics who have panned him over the years.

Locations: Devlin's Apartment (interior and exterior): Peninsula Heights, 93 Albert Embankment, Vauxhall, London, SE1.

Maxwell's Burial Site: Kensal Green Cemetery, Harrow Road, London, NW10.

Solomon's House (exterior and interior): 8 Cheyne Walk, Chelsea, London.

Peninsula Heights on the Thames embankment doubles as the home of Devlin (Ian Hendry). Vincent Price (as Edward Lionheart) throws himself from its balcony into the Thames.

Kensel Green Cemetery in North London dates back to the nineteenth century and boasts one of the world's finest collection of monuments belonging to royalty and aristocracy. In the film it is the burial place of Maxwell (Michael Hordern) and the setting when Hector Snipe's body (Dennis Price) is dragged by a horse in front of the mourners, to horrible effect.

8 Cheyne Walk in Chelsea doubles as the home where Solomon (Jack

Left — Theatre of Blood: Peninsula Heights, 93 Albert Embankment, Vauxhall, London, doubles as the home of Devlin (Ian Hendry), where Edward Lionheart (Vincent Price) throws himself from the balcony. (Photograph by the author.)
Right — Theatre of Blood: 8 Cheyne Walk, Chelsea, London, doubles as the home of Solomon (Jack Hawkins), where he suffocates his wife (Diana Dors) to death. (Photograph by the author.)

Theatre of Blood: The body of Hector Snipe (Dennis Price) being dragged behind a horse, to horrible effect, in front of a group of mourners, was filmed at Kensal Green Cemetery, Harrow Road, London. (Photograph by the author.)

Hawkins), deceived by Edward Lionheart that his wife Diana Dors has been having an affair, suffocates her to death.

Theatre of Death
Pennea Productions (1966)

Cast: Christopher Lee, Jenny Till, Lelia Goldoni, Julian Glover, Ivor Dean, Evelyn Laye
Screenplay: Roger Marshall, Ellis Kadison
Producer: Michael Smedley-Aston
Director: Sam Gallu

Vampire-like murders in Paris are eventually connected with a Grand Guignol Theatre.

Studio: Elstree Studios, Borehamwood, Hertfordshire.
Location: French Le Theatre du Grand Guignol (auditorium): Lyric Theatre, King Street, Hammersmith, London, W6 0QL.

Doubling as the interior of the Grand Guignol Theatre is Hammersmith's Lyric Theatre.

To the Devil a Daughter
Hammer Films (1976)

Cast: Richard Widmark, Christopher Lee, Nastassja Kinski, Denholm Elliott, Honor Blackman, Michael Goodliffe, Anthony Valentine, Derek Francis, Brian Wilde, Frances De La Tour
Screenplay: Chris Wicking
Producer: Roy Skeggs
Director: Peter Sykes

A girl is promised to a group of Satanists who want to dedicate her to the Devil.

Studio: Elstree Studios, Borehamwood, Hertfordshire.
Location: Mausoleum: The Dashwood Mausoleum, The Dashwood Estate, West Wycombe Park, Buckinghamshire, HP14 3AJ.

Built in 1765 as a final resting place for members of the Dashwood family, the vast, roofless, hexagon-shaped mausoleum (built of Portland stone and

To the Devil a Daughter: The climax of the film, in which Christopher Lee plans to give the soul of Nastassja Kinski to the Devil, was filmed at the Dashwood Mausoleum, West Wycombe Park, Buckinghamshire. Courtesy of Simon Flynn.

To the Devil a Daughter: The Dashwood Mausoleum, West Wycombe Park, Buckinghamshire, features during the climax. Courtesy of Simon Flynn.*

flint) was used to dramatic effect at the climax of this movie as Christopher Lee plans to give the soul of Nastassia Kinski to the Devil.

The Tomb of Ligeia
Anglo-Amalgamated Productions (1964)

Cast: Vincent Price, Elizabeth Shepherd, John Westbrook, Oliver Johnston, Derek Francis, Richard Vernon, Frank Thornton
Screenplay: Robert Towne
Producer-Director: Roger Corman

A brooding Victorian metamorphoses his dead wife into a cat, then into the beautiful Lady Rowena.

Studio: Shepperton Studios, Middlesex.
Location: The Abbey (exterior): Castle Acre Priory, Stocks Green, Castle Acre, Nr. Swaffham, Norfolk, PE32 2AE.

Playing the half-derelict home of eccentric Verden Fell (Vincent Price) is Castle Acre Priory in Norfolk (see the chapter "Locations — In Detail" for a more in-depth look).

*"The Dashwood Mausoleum is eerie and very quiet. Viewing the inside of the mausoleum I saw the tombs, and you can see the attention to detail on the inner walls."— Simon Flynn

This was the second of only two horror films directed in England by American Roger Corman. The first, *The Masque of the Red Death* (1964), was not shot on location.

Trog
Herman Cohen Productions (1970)

Cast: Joan Crawford, Michael Gough, Bernard Kay, Kim Braden, David Griffin, John Hamill, Thorley Walters, Robert Hutton, David Warbeck
Screenplay: Aben Kandel
Producer: Herman Cohen
Director: Freddie Francis

An apeman, discovered living in a cave, is captured and subjected to experiments conducted by a woman scientist.

Location: Brockton Research Centre (exterior): New Lodge, Drift Road, Winkfield, Windsor, Berkshire, SL4 4RQ.

Doubling as the Brockton Research Centre where Joan Crawford's experiments on an apeman go horribly wrong is New Lodge in Berkshire.

Trog: New Lodge, Drift Road, Winkfield, Windsor, Berkshire, doubles as the Brockton research center, where Joan Crawford experiments on a living prehistoric apeman. Courtesy of Simon Flynn.

28 Days Later: Waverley Abbey, Nr. Farnham, Surrey, appears briefly in the movie when Cillian Murphy, Naome Harris and Brendan Gleeson decide to hide within its derelict walls. Courtesy of Simon Flynn.*

28 Days Later
Canal+ (2002)

Cast: Cillian Murphy, Naome Harris, Christopher Eccleston, Megan Burns, Brendan Gleeson
Screenplay: Alex Garland
Producer: Andrew Macdonald
Director: Danny Boyle

A powerful virus is unleashed, locking those infected into a permanent state of murderous rage.

Locations: Ruined Abbey Sequence: Waverley Abbey, Nr. Farnham, Surrey.

Country House Sequences (exterior and interior): Trafalgar Park, Nr. Salisbury, Wiltshire, SP5 3QR.

Appearing briefly when the group (Cillian Murphy, Naome Harris, Brendan Gleeson) decides to hide within its derelict walls from the virus is

---
*"The ruins are certainly worth a visit."— Simon Flynn

Waverley Abbey, which was founded in the Eleventh Century. Not a lot of the structure exists today, just the bare bones of the refectory and a few transept walls. However the site does still manage to create an atmosphere of something grander.

The climax of the film, featuring Christopher Eccleston, was filmed at the lavish stately home Trafalgar Park, built in 1733.

Twins of Evil
Hammer Films (1971)

Cast: Peter Cushing, Dennis Price, Isobel Black, Mary Collinson, Madeleine Collinson, Kathleen Byron, David Warbeck, Damien Thomas, Alex Scott, Luan Peters, Harvey Hall
Screenplay: Tudor Gates
Producers: Harry Fine, Michael Style
Director: John Hough

Identical twins become victims of a vampire cult.

Studio: Pinewood Studios, Buckinghamshire.
Location: Woodland: Black Park, Black Park Road, Wexham, Buckinghamshire, SL3 6DR.

All woodland sequences featuring the vicious witch-hunters, led by Peter Cushing's fanatical Gustav Weil were shot at Black Park in Buckinghamshire.

The Vampire Lovers
Hammer Films (1970)

Cast: Ingrid Pitt, Peter Cushing, Pippa Steele, Madeleine Smith, George Cole, Dawn Addams, Douglas Wilmer, Kate O'Mara, Jon Finch, John Forbes-Robertson, Harvey Hall, Ferdy Mayne, Janet Key
Screenplay: Tudor Gates, Harry Fine, Michael Style
Producers: Harry Fine, Michael Style
Director: Roy Ward Baker

A voluptuous lesbian vampire seduces many a young, pretty female victim.

Studio: Elstree Studios, Borehamwood, Hertfordshire.
Locations: Spielsdorf's Mansion House (exterior): Moor Park Mansion, Rickmansworth, Hertfordshire, WD3 1QN.

Morton's Mansion House (exterior): Wall Hall Mansion, Church Lane, Aldenham, Watford, Hertfordshire, WD2 8AT.

The Vampire Lovers: Wall Hall Mansion, Church Lane, Aldenham, Watford, Hertfordshire, doubles as the home of Morton (George Cole). Courtesy of Ruth Potter.

The Grade 1-listed Moor Park Mansion (now part of a golf club) was designed in the eighteenth century, and is a magnificent example of classic English architecture. It appears at the opening of the movie as the grand home of General Spielsdorf (Peter Cushing), who unknowingly invites the vampire Carmilla (Ingrid Pitt) into his house.

Wall Hall Mansion in Hertfordshire, now being re-developed into apartments, doubles as the home of Morton (George Cole).

Vampyres
Lurco Films (1974)

Cast: Marianne Morris, Murray Brown, Sally Faulkner, Brian Deacon, Michael Byrne, Anulka, Gerald Case, Bessie Love
Screenplay: D. Daubeney
Producer: Brian Smedley-Aston
Director: Joseph Larraz

Two murdered lesbian hitch-hikers return as vampires and take their revenge on male drivers.

Locations: Manor House (exterior and interior): Oakley Court Hotel, Windsor Road, Water Oakley, Windsor, SL4 5UR.

The Church (exterior): St. Mary the Virgin, Village Road, Denham Village, Denham, Buckinghamshire, UB9 5BH.

The lair of the two lesbian vampires (Marianne Morris and Anulka) is the gothic Oakley Court in Windsor.

Doubling as the church is St. Mary the Virgin in Denham Village. Standing almost beside the church in Denham Village is the former home of Sir John Mills, who lived there up until his death in 2005.

Vampyres: Doubling in the film as "The Church" is St. Mary the Virgin, Village Road, Denham Village, Buckinghamshire. Courtesy of Simon Flynn.*

Vault of Horror
Amicus Films (1973)

Cast: Terry-Thomas, Glynis Johns, Curt Jurgens, Daniel Massey, Anna Massey, Dawn Addams, Denholm Elliott, Michael Pratt, John Forbes-Robertson, Michael Craig, Edward Judd, Arthur Mullard, Tom Baker, Roy Evans
Screenplay: Milton Subotsky
Producers: Milton Subotsky, Max J. Rosenberg
Director: Roy Ward Baker

Five men are trapped in a tower block and tell stories of murder, vampirism and voodoo.

Studio: Twickenham Studios, Middlesex.
Location: Tower Block (exterior): Millbank Tower, Millbank, Westminster, London, SW1.

*"*The church is very peaceful and tranquil. You can instantly recognize that* Vampyres *was shot there."— Simon Flynn*

A highly impressive tower block, Millbank Tower in Westminster, can be seen during the opening credits as the tower where five men (Terry-Thomas, Curt Jurgens, Daniel Massey, Michael Craig, Tom Baker) get trapped and tell their horror stories.

Village of the Damned
Metro-Goldwyn-Mayer (1960)

Cast: George Sanders, Barbara Shelley, Michael Gwynn, Martin Stephens, Laurence Naismith, Jenny Laird, Bernard Archard, Peter Vaughan, Richard Vernon
Screenplay: Stirling Silliphant, Wolf Rilla, Geoffrey Barclay
Producer: Ronald Kinnoch
Director: Wolf Rilla

Children born simultaneously in an English village prove to be super-intelligent and deadly beings from another planet.

Left — Vault of Horror: Doubling as the tower block where five men (Terry-Thomas, Curt Jurgens, Daniel Massey, Michael Craig, Tom Baker) get trapped and tell horror stories is Millbank Tower, Millbank, Westminster, London. (Photograph by the author.) *Right — Village of the Damned*: Doubling as Midwich Village is Letchmore Heath, Nr. Watford, Hertfordshire. Courtesy of Ruth Potter.

Top: Village of the Damned: Aldenham House, Butterfly Lane, Elstree, Borehamwood, Hertfordshire, doubles as Midwich Manor, home to Professor Zellaby (George Sanders). Courtesy of Ruth Potter. *Bottom: Village of the Damned*: St. John the Baptist, Church Lane, Aldenham, Hertfordshire, doubles as Midwich Church during the opening credits. Courtesy of Ruth Potter.

Studio: MGM Studios, Borehamwood, Hertfordshire.
Locations: Midwich Manor (exterior): Aldenham House, The Haberdashers' Aske's Boys' School, Butterfly Lane, Elstree, Borehamwood, Hertfordshire, WD6 3AF.
Midwich Village: Letchmore Heath, Aldenham, Nr. Watford, Hertfordshire.
Midwich Church (exterior): St. John the Baptist, Church Lane, Aldenham, Hertfordshire, WD25 8BR.

Aldenham House, previously a seventeenth century private manor house, but now part of the Haberdashers' Aske's Boys' School in Hertfordshire, doubles as Midwich Manor, home to Professor Gordon Zellaby (George Sanders).

Letchmore Heath, complete with its sixteenth century cottages and seventeenth century inn, doubles as Midwich Village in the movie. The twelfth century Aldenham Church (St. John the Baptist) doubles as Midwich Church during the opening credits.

Virgin Witch
Tigon Films (1971)

Cast: Ann Michelle, Vicki Michelle, Neil Hallett, James Chase, Patricia Haines, Keith Buckley, Paula Wright
Screenplay: Klaus Vogel
Producer: Ralph Solomons
Director: Ray Austin

Two girls go to London to become models but get involved in Satanism when one of them, a psychic lesbian, tries to make her girlfriend a witch.

Location: Wychwold House (exterior and interior): Admiral's Walk, Mill Lane, Pirbright, Nr. Woking, Surrey, GU24.

A large private house, Admiral's Walk in Surrey, doubles as Wychwold, where Ann and Vicki Michelle get mixed up in Satanism.

The Watcher in the Woods
Walt Disney (1980)

Cast: Bette Davis, Caroll Baker, David McCallum, Lynn-Holly Johnson, Ian Bannen, Richard Pasco, Kyle Richards, Frances Cuka, Benedict Taylor, Georgina Hale
Screenplay: Brian Clemens, Harry Spalding, Rosemary Anne Sisson

The Watcher in the Woods: Doubling as the home of the eccentric Keller (Ian Bannen) is Ettington Park Hotel, Alderminster, Stratford-upon-Avon, Warwickshire. Courtesy of Ettington Park Hotel.

Producer: Tom Leetch
Director: John Hough

An American family buys a country home in Britain, but finds that it is haunted by the spirit of a young child, the missing daughter of the owner.

Studio: Pinewood Studios, Buckinghamshire.
Locations: The Aylwood House (exterior and interior): St. Huberts, St. Huberts Lane, Gerrards Cross, Buckinghamshire.
Keller's Mansion (exterior): Ettington Park Hotel, Alderminster, Stratford-upon-Avon, Warwickshire, CV37 8BU.

A private country estate St. Huberts in Buckinghamshire doubles as the large house owned by Mrs. Aylwood (Bette Davis). Ettington Park Hotel in Stratford-upon-Avon appears as the home of the eccentric. Keller (Ian Bannen).

The Wicker Man
British Lion Film Corporation (1973)

Cast: Edward Woodward, Britt Ekland, Christopher Lee, Ingrid Pitt, Diane Cilento, Aubrey Morris, Walter Carr, Geraldine Cowper
Screenplay: Anthony Shaffer
Producer: Peter Snell
Director: Robin Hardy

A detective investigating the disappearance of a child on a remote Scottish island is slowly drawn into a web of intrigue by the inhabitants, who are worshippers of a strange and sinister cult.

Locations: Green Man Inn (interior): The Ellangowan Hotel, Dumfries, Scotland.

Green Man Inn (exterior): The Cally Estate Offices, Gatehouse of Fleet, Dumfries & Galloway, Scotland.

Summerisle Schoolhouse (exterior and interior): Church Cottage, Anwoth, Dumfries & Galloway, Scotland.

Summerisle Churchyard: Old Kirkyard, Anwoth, Dumfries & Galloway, Scotland.

Lord Summerisle's Castle (exterior): Culzean Castle, Maybole, South Ayrshire, Scotland, KA19 8LE.

Lord Summerisle's Castle (interior): Lochinch Castle, Stranraer, Dumfries & Galloway, Scotland, DG9.

End Sequence with The Wicker Man: Burrow Head cliffs, Burrow Head, Dumfries & Galloway, Scotland.

The interior of the Green Man Inn, where Edward Woodward rents a room, is actually the Ellangowen Hotel in Dumfries, Scotland. The exterior of the inn are the Cally Estate Offices in Gatehouse of Fleet.

Doubling as the Summerisle Schoolhouse, where, to the horror of Woodward, Diane Cilento is teaching obscene lessons to young children in the classroom, is the tiny Church Cottage in Anwoth. Directly opposite this is the derelict Old Kirkyard, which appears in the film as the rather strange Summerisle Churchyard.

Culzean, a beautiful, romantic eighteenth century castle, perched on a cliff edge (see "Locations—In Detail" for a more in-depth look), doubles as the exterior of Lord Summerisle's (Christopher Lee) home. The interiors were Lochinch Castle, built in 1864, and now the home of the earl and countess of Stair.

The end sequence in which Woodward is burned alive in a gigantic wicker man was filmed on the cliffs at Burrow Head in Scotland. For this scene, two giant wicker men were built. The legs of one, used for the final shot, can still be seen standing on the cliff's edge.

"The powerful climax of the film with the magnificent and quite terrifying Wicker Man—of which I hold one of the only remaining pieces—was made even more dramatic by its unforgettable and striking location, Burrow Head cliffs in Scotland."—Christopher Lee

Witchcraft
Lippert Pictures (1964)

Cast: Lon Chaney, Jr., Jack Hedley, Marie Ney, Jill Dixon, David Weston, Diane Clare, Yvette Rees, Victor Brooks, Marianne Stone
Screenplay: Harry Spalding
Producers: Robert Lippert, Jack Parsons
Director: Don Sharp

A family of witches uses supernatural rites to take revenge on their longtime enemies.

Studio: Shepperton Studios, Middlesex.
Location: The Lanier House (exterior): Oakley Court Hotel, Windsor Road, Water Oakley, Windsor, SL4 5UR.

Oakley Court doubles as the Lanier House, the ancestral estate of Morgan Whitlock (Lon Chaney, Jr.).

The Witches
Jim Henson Productions (1990)

Cast: Anjelica Huston, Mai Zetterling, Jasen Fisher, Jane Horrocks, Rowan Atkinson, Bill Paterson, Brenda Blethyn, Jim Carter
Screenplay: Allan Scott
Producer: Mark Shivas
Director: Nicolas Roeg

A young boy stumbles across a witch convention and sets out to stop them, even after they have turned him into a mouse.

Studio: Bray Studios, Windsor, Berkshire.
Location: Hotel Excelsior (exterior): The Headland Hotel, Fistral Beach, Newquay, Cornwall, TR7 1EW.

Featured as the Hotel Excelsior, the venue of a secret witches' convention, is the Headland Hotel, a rather impressive structure, built in 1897, and sitting on a cliff's edge in Newquay, Cornwall.

Witchfinder General
Tigon Films (1968)

Cast: Vincent Price, Ian Ogilvy, Rupert Davies, Patrick Wymark, Wilfred Brambell, Robert Russell, Nicky Henson, Hilary Dwyer, Tony Selby, Godfrey James, Maggie Kimberly

Top: Witchfinder General: Doubling as the exterior of Brandeston church is St. John the Evangelist, Rushford, Nr. Thetford, Norfolk. (Photograph by the author.) *Bottom: Witchfinder General*: St. John the Evangelist, Rushford, Nr. Thetford, Norfolk, also doubles as the interior of Brandeston Church. (Photograph by the author.)

132 *Witchfinder General*

***Witchfinder General*:** Doubling as the Parsonage, home to John Lowes (Rupert Davies) and his daughter Sarah (Hilary Dwyer), is the Parsonage at St. John the Evangelist, Rushford, Nr. Thetford, Norfolk. (Photograph by the author.)

Screenplay: Michael Reeves, Tom Baker
Producers: Arnold Miller, Philip Waddilove, Louis M. Heyward
Director: Michael Reeves

A sadistic witch-hunter, Matthew Hopkins, scours the countryside using brutal torture in order to extract confessions.

Locations: Brandeston Church and Parsonage (exteriors and interiors): St. John the Evangelist (Church of England), Rushford, Nr. Thetford, Norfolk.

Brandeston Hall (exterior): Kentwell Hall, Long Melford, Suffolk, CO10 9BA.

Coastal Sequence: Dunwich, Suffolk.

Lavenham: Lavenham Market Square, Lavenham, Suffolk.

Lavenham Castle (exterior and interior): Orford Castle, Orford, Suffolk, IP12 21J.

The fourteenth century church and parsonage in Rushford, Norfolk (St. John the Evangelist), doubles as Brandeston Church, home of John Lowes (Rupert Davies) and his daughter Sarah (Hilary Dwyer).

Brandeston Hall is actually Kentwell Hall (see "Locations — In Detail" for a more in-depth look). It is here that witch-hunter Hopkins (Vincent Price) swims some of his victims, including John Lowes, in its moat.

The sequence with Richard Marshall (Ian Ogilvy) on horseback, standing before a raging sea, was shot on location at Dunwich in Suffolk, a coastal village with dramatic chalk cliffs.

Lavenham, a beautiful medieval market town with Tudor-style buildings, was a stomping ground for the real Matthew Hopkins, and appears here when a woman, Elizabeth Clark (Maggie Kimberly), is burned alive in the market square.

The end sequence in which Hopkins takes Marshall and Sarah Lowes (Dwyer) to Lavenham Castle to be tortured, but ends up being axed to death himself, is actually Orford Castle in Suffolk (see the chapter "Locations — In Detail" for a more in-depth look).

The Studios

This chapter looks at some of the studios that have played a part in the production of horror films over the last 70 years.

BRAY STUDIOS
Water Oakley, Windsor, Berkshire

Films: *The Brides of Dracula* (1960), *The Curse of Frankenstein* (1957), *Dracula* (1958), *Frankenstein Created Woman* (1966), *The Hole* (2001), *The Hound of the Baskervilles* (1959), *The Mummy* (1959), *The Phantom of the Opera* (1962), *The Plague of the Zombies* (1965), *The Quatermass Xperiment* (1955), *The Witches* (1990)

Bray Studios was once a splendid private residence known as Down Place. A seventeenth-century country mansion, it was owned originally by Jacob Tonson. He was an eminent bookseller of the day who attracted noblemen and gentlemen to his home and formed the famous Kit-Kat Club with the Earl of Dorset at its head. The club had 39 members who were distinguished for their rank, learning, and wit, and many held important government positions.

Down Place remained a private residence until 1949 when it was sold and, shortly afterwards, became Bray Studios. The character and mystique of the original house remain today, along (it is claimed) with the resident ghost, known as The Blue Lady.

Bray Studios will always be associated with Hammer Film Productions.

The original House of Hammer had been started in the 1930s by Spanish-French Enrique Carreras and William Hinds, an ex-actor who went under the name of Will Hammer.

At Bray Studios, Hammer would be run by Carreras, his two sons James and Michael, Hinds and *his* son Anthony.

In the early 1950s Hammer Films produced low-budget versions of successful radio series such as *The Man in Black*, *Life with the Lyons*, and *PC 49*.

In the mid–1950s, James Carreras secured the rights to television's *The Quatermass Experiment*. The success of this science fiction film was so phenomenal that the company decided to concentrate on the remunerative horror formula. After *Quatermass 2* in 1957 (filmed at New Elstree Studios), they turned their attention to *The Curse of Frankenstein*. This film was to set the style for the Hammer House of Horror, and launched the company — and its stars, Peter Cushing & Christopher Lee — on a long and profitable run. Filled with lurid colors with lashings of blood, this brand of entertainment seemed just what the British cinema-going public was waiting for.

During their peak years, Hammer was producing eight films a year. Their success in the home market and in the United States enabled Hammer to claim the distinction of being Britain's most consistently profitable film company.

However, by the mid–1960s, film production was declining in Great Britain, and Bray, in common with a number of other studios, was in difficulties. Hammer continued to make movies at other locations; their last film at Bray was produced in 1966.

Since this time the studio has changed hands several times, but still continues as a home for film productions, and even horror films, like the disturbing recent chiller, *The Hole* (2001).

Bushey Film Studios
Melbourne Road, Bushey, Hertfordshire
Film: *Castle Sinister* (1932)

Bushey Film Studios, situated on Melbourne Road in Bushey, Hertfordshire, is Britain's oldest surviving, fully intact, "glasshouse" film studio, and perhaps the oldest in the world.

"Glasshouse" refers to the structure that resembles a greenhouse on the top of the building. This is where films were shot using natural light before the introduction of lamps for lighting. The studio had a revolving floor so that the set could be moved around as the position of the sun changed.

It was built in 1913 by eminent portrait painter Sir Hubert von Herkomer on the grounds of his fairytale mansion, Lululaund. His first commercial film at the studio was *The Old Wood Carver* (1913). Herkomer died in 1914.

The studio lived on, though, taken over by several different film companies. In 1932 the first-ever British horror film, *Castle Sinister*, was produced there. It was however a poorly received movie which rarely sees the light of day today.

Some of the more notable films made there included *Black Memory* (1947) with Sidney James and Michael Medwin; *The Greed of William Hart* (1948), directed by Oswald Mitchell, starring Tod Slaughter; and *Bless 'em All* (1949) with Max Bygraves. The studio was also used for a period by the Children's Film Foundation.

Castle Sinister: The first ever British sound horror film was made entirely at Bushey Film Studios, Melbourne Road, Bushey, Hertfordshire. (Photograph by the author.)

To some, the old "glasshouse" studio seemed an eerie place, and it was said by many to be haunted. Some refused to work in it late at night. Others who did reported hearing footsteps and other noises that they found unaccountable.

One construction manager, a very down-to-earth man who was working late one evening building a film set, was positive that he saw a woman, wearing a long dress, walk across the studio and go behind some standing scenery. Some believe that it was the ghost of Lulu, the second wife of Sir Hubert von Herkomer.

Another ghost said to haunt the building is that of an actor who is believed to have committed suicide in a dressing room, many years ago.

Bushey ceased working as a film studio in the 1960s. The building itself still stands today, converted into business offices.

EALING STUDIOS
Ealing Green, Ealing, London
Written by Brian Holland

Films: *Dead of Night* (1945), *Half Light* (2006), *Shaun of the Dead* (2004)

***Dead of Night*:** The first ever British compendium horror film was made at the old Ealing Studios, Ealing Green, Ealing, London. (Photograph by the author.)

Ealing Studios is renowned for some of the best-loved British film comedies. It celebrated its 100th birthday in 2002, making it the oldest film studio in the world still in production.

The studio was founded in 1902 by Will Barker, one of the earliest proponents of the moving picture camera. In the early 1930s Basil Dean, the owner of Associated Talking Pictures, took over from Barker. He was joined in 1938 by Michael Balcon as head of production.

One of the great names in British entertainment, Ealing Studios is famous around the world as the home of the great Ealing comedies of the 1940s and '50s, some of the greatest comedy classics the British film industry has ever seen. A selection includes the likes of *Whisky Galore* (1948), *Kind Hearts and Coronets* (1949), *The Lavender Hill Mob* (1951), and possibly their most famous comedy *The Ladykillers* (1955). Yet at the same time the studio was also responsible for some great thrillers, action, and dramatic films such as *The Cruel Sea* (1953), the beautifully filmed (in color) *Scott of the Antarctic* (1948), and the first British compendium horror chiller, *Dead of Night* (1945).

The studio was taken over by the BBC in 1959 and they spent the next twenty years there creating television productions such as *Colditz*, *The Singing Detective*, *Fortunes of War*, and even *Monty Python's Flying Circus*.

In recent years Ealing Studios has accommodated such high-profile films as *An Ideal Husband* (1999), *Notting Hill* (1999), *Star Wars — Episode II* (2002), *The Importance of Being Earnest* (2002), *Half Light* (2006), and the smash hit horror comedy *Shaun of the Dead* (2004).

Ealing is presently redeveloping its 3.8-acre site in West London at the cost of £50 million and work is already underway to complete the new state-of-the-art film and television studios.

According to Sean Hinton, managing director of the studios, "[We said we would do] two things when we bought the studio in 2000. Firstly, rebuild and redevelop the studios so that it is a facility that would serve film and television production for another 100 years, and secondly to re-launch Ealing Studios as a production company as it was in the 1940s and '50s in the Hollywood sense."

ELSTREE STUDIOS
Shenley Road, Borehamwood, Hertfordshire

Films: *The Abominable Dr. Phibes* (1971), *The Anniversary* (1968), *The Awakening* (1980), *A Clockwork Orange* (1971), *Demons of the Mind* (1972), *The Devil Rides Out* (1968), *Dracula A.D. 1972* (1971), *Fear in the Night* (1971), *Frankenstein and the Monster from Hell* (1972), *Frankenstein Must Be Destroyed* (1969), *The Legend of Hell House* (1973), *Lust for a Vampire* (1970), *The Monster Club* (1980), *The Nanny* (1965), *Night of the Demon* (1957), *Omen III—The Final Conflict* (1981), *The Satanic Rites of Dracula* (1972), *Secret Ceremony* (1969), *The Shining* (1980), *Taste the Blood of Dracula* (1970), *Theatre of Death* (1966), *To the Devil a Daughter* (1976), *The Vampire Lovers* (1970)

Elstree Film Studios has a long and very distinguished history. The present facilities are built on land originally purchased in 1925, to locate a "silent" studio constructed one year later. At that time, Alfred Hitchcock was engaged as a staff director there and was responsible for a number of films, including the first British talkie, *Blackmail* (1929).

During the pre-war years, the studios undertook pioneering work in color films and produced the first French talkie and the first multi-lingual film. It also launched a number of pre-war movie acting careers, including those of Charles Laughton, Laurence Olivier, Robert Newton, Vivien Leigh and Maureen O'Hara.

A few years later, Warner Bros. purchased a 25 percent share in the parent company, ABPC, and the studio was largely rebuilt before re-opening in 1948. Their first major post-war movies were Hitchcock's *Stage Fright* (1950) with Marlene Dietrich and *The Hasty Heart* (1949) starring none other than future American president Ronald Reagan.

Post-war careers launched at Elstree included those of Richard Harris, Audrey Hepburn and Richard Todd.

The 1950s and '60s saw productions such as *Moby Dick* (1956) with Gregory Peck, *Kings Rhapsody* (1955) with Errol Flynn, *The Dam Busters* (1954), *Look Back in Anger* (1959) with Richard Burton, and *The Naked Edge* (1961) featuring the final performance of Gary Cooper.

Elstree was also responsible for hit TV series such as *The Avengers* with Patrick Macnee and *The Saint* with Roger Moore. It was also the base for film director Stanley Kubrick, who shot most of his films at the studio, including *A Clockwork Orange* and the horror thriller *The Shining*.

Between 1959 and 1976 Hammer Films produced 39 films at Elstree, including *The Nanny* (1965) with Bette Davis, *The Devil Rides Out* (1968) with Christopher Lee, and *Frankenstein and the Monster from Hell* (1972) with Peter Cushing.

The studio was busy throughout the 1970s and '80s with productions such as *Murder on the Orient Express* (1974), the Bond film *Never Say Never Again* (1983) with Sean Connery, the original *Star Wars* trilogy, and Spielberg's *Indiana Jones* trilogy.

In 1986, Cannon purchased the studios, sold off the film library and announced closure plans in 1988. This prompted a successful "Save Our Studios" campaign which resulted in worldwide media coverage, a 700-strong audience at a public meeting and nearly 30,000 petition signatures. It was successful in enlisting the support of Spielberg, George Lucas, Lord Attenborough, and a host of stars including Peter Cushing—who even offered to lie down in front of the bulldozers!

Hertsmere Borough Council bought the studio in 1996 and it soon reopened for business and attracted numerous television productions, including a version of *Jane Eyre*, interiors for the long-running *Last of the Summer Wine*, and an adaptation of *Wuthering Heights*.

As an added note of interest, during the studio's heyday the people and pubs of Borehamwood became accustomed to seeing Yul Brynner and Errol Flynn sharing a pint at the Red Lion, directly opposite the studios (now a McDonald's), or Harrison Ford strolling along the street to the news agents. It was a strange mixture of high glamour and a fish-and-chips shop English town.

Alfred Hitchcock, while under contract at the studios, used to drink regularly at the Plough public house on the High Street in Elstree. The place is now known as The East, an Oriental restaurant.

Abbots Mead, a house on Barnet Lane in Elstree, was for many years the home of Stanley Kubrick while he produced and directed his movies at the studios.

In recent years, twelve acres of the Elstree Studios site was sold off, and several of its sound stages flattened. In its place was built a Tesco supermarket. The area where *Star Wars* was filmed is now displaced by the frozen food aisle.

LIME GROVE STUDIOS
Lime Grove, Shepherd's Bush, London

Film: *The Ghoul* (1933)

Lime Grove Studios was a studio complex built by the Gaumont Film Company in 1915, and situated in a street named Lime Grove in Shepherd's Bush, London.

It was described by Gaumont as "the finest studio in Great Britain and the first building ever put up in this country solely for the production of films."

The studios prospered under Gaumont and, later, Gainsborough Pictures. Not long after the start of World War II, they were bought by J. Arthur Rank and became a home on many occasions to the Ealing Comedies. The famous British film *The Wicked Lady* with James Mason and Margaret Lockwood was made at Lime Grove.

In 1949, as the BBC built their Television Centre at nearby White City, they bought Lime Grove as a "temporary measure" and began converting it for television use.

Lime Grove would become home to many BBC television shows over the next forty two years, including *Nineteen Eighty Four* with Peter Cushing and *Quatermass II* in the 1950s, and early episodes of *Doctor Who* in the 1960s.

In 1991, the BBC decided to consolidate its other London television production at BBC Television Centre and close its other studios including Lime Grove. So in July 1991 the studios, which had been a place of film and television production for 76 years, were closed forever.

Shortly after, they were put on the market and eventually were bought by a development company which demolished the studio and redeveloped the area for residential housing.

Such a shame then that the studio that brought us *The Ghoul* with Boris Karloff in 1933 should become victim to the demolition men.

MGM FILM STUDIOS
Elstree Way, Borehamwood, Hertfordshire

Films: *Children of the Damned* (1964), *The Haunting* (1963), *Village of the Damned* (1960)

Metro-Goldwyn-Mayer established a British operation at Denham Film Studios in 1936. In 1948 they took control of the former Amalgamated Studios site on Elstree Way in Borehamwood, Hertfordshire.

Productions made at the MGM-British studios include the classic horror *The Haunting* in 1963, and other famous movies like *Where Eagles Dare* (1969) and *2001: A Space Odyssey* (1968).

2001 has been cited as one of the primary causes behind the closing down of the studio, due to the fact that Stanley Kubrick's film occupied more and more of the available studio space — eventually using all of it — for almost two years, thus rendering the facilities massively unprofitable in the long run.

The studio remained in operation until 1970, one of the last shows in production being the cult TV series *UFO*. At that time the studio merged with the EMI facility (commonly known as Elstree Studios) and therefore the site was cleared.

NETTLEFOLD STUDIOS
Hurst Grove, Walton-on-Thames, Surrey

Films: *Mother Riley Meets the Vampire* (1952), *The Mystery of the Mary Celeste* (1935)

In 1895, magic lantern operator Cecil Hepworth leased a house, The Rosary, in Hurst Grove, Walton-on-Thames, for £36 a year, and built a small outdoor stage in his garden for the production of films.

The first films made at his new studio were *The Egg-Laying Man* (1896) and *The Eccentric Dancer*. His filming of Queen Victoria's funeral procession in 1901 and the coronation procession of Edward VII shortly afterwards were remarkable achievements for the time.

Hepworth then went on to make an ambitious 800-foot film, *Alice in Wonderland* (1903), breaking him away from the 50 foot tradition. By the early part of the twentieth century, the Hepworth studio was making approximately 100 films a year.

By the 1930s it had been given the name Nettlefold Studios, and was being rented out regularly to other independent companies, one of which was Hammer Films, who made *The Mystery of the Mary Celeste* with Bela Lugosi there.

In 1937, Nettlefold launched a new stage abutted to the rear of the existing studio after purchasing a large mid–Victorian house, The Croft, and building a new sound stage with water tank on the land. That same year also saw the arrival of music hall artists Arthur Lucan and his wife, Kitty McShane, alias Old Mother Riley and her wayward daughter Kitty. The Mother Riley character would appear in a series of fifteen low-budget comedy films, seven of which were produced at Nettlefold, ending in 1952 with *Mother Riley Meets the Vampire*, which would mark the return of Bela Lugosi to the studio.

The 1950s saw films produced with the occasional star performance, including *Svengali* (1954) with Donald Wolfit.

Thanks to the launch of a third commercial television channel, ITV, Nettlefold would become home to their first television series, *The Adventures of Robin Hood*, starring Richard Greene in the title role. The leafy surroundings of Walton-on-Thames were perfect for recreating Sherwood Forest; the Sheriff of Nottingham's castle was built on a plot of land behind Bridge Street. The series was the brainchild of American Hannah Weinstein, who fled to England as a refugee from the McCarthy anti–Communist witch-hunt. Weinstein established her own company at Walton, Sapphire Films.

By the end of the 1950s, Nettlefold's fortunes had completely declined due to the popularity of television and a lack of production funding for low to medium-budget films. This once unique studio was never able to expand further or gather a strong personality, and with larger modern studios claiming the lion's share of work, Nettlefold closed in 1961. The majority of the equipment was sold to Shepperton. Shortly after this, the studio's sound stages and buildings were demolished and the area redeveloped to create a new shopping center. One small part of the studio which does still exist, and stands today (on Hurst Grove) in memory of Nettlefold, is now called the Playhouse Theatre.

PINEWOOD STUDIOS
Pinewood Road, Iver Heath, Buckinghamshire
Written by Sally-Anne Ryan

Films: *The Beast in the Cellar* (1970), *Blood on Satan's Claw* (1970), *Carry On Screaming* (1966), *The Descent* (2005), *Doomwatch* (1972), *Dracula Has Risen from the Grave* (1968), *Frankenstein: The True Story* (1973), *Frenzy* (1972), *The Ghoul* (1974), *Hands of the Ripper* (1971), *I Don't Want to Be Born* (1975), *Interview with the Vampire* (1994), *Island of Terror* (1966), *Jack the Ripper* (1988), *Legend of the Werewolf* (1974), *The Mummy Returns* (2001), *Night of the Big Heat* (1967), *Nothing but the Night* (1972), *Peeping Tom* (1960), *Twins of Evil* (1971), *The Watcher in the Woods* (1980)

Before becoming the world-famous Pinewood Studios, this studio was a private residence called Heatherden Hall. Owned by Lt. Col. Grant Morden, a Canadian financier and MP for Chiswick and Brentford, it was substantially changed into a magnificent showplace, with a ballroom, private squash court and Turkish bath. It soon became a private meeting place for politicians and diplomats. In 1934 Morden died and Heatherden Hall was bought at auction by Sir Charles Boot, a Sheffield building tycoon with movie ambitions. The name Pinewood came from the many pine trees that grew on the grounds.

When Boot met the Methodist and flour magnate, J. Arthur Rank, in 1935, they became partners in the studio project and set about making Pinewood the great studio it is today. Construction of the studio began in December of that year and was completed nine months later, with producers booking months in advance to use the facilities. The first film to be made entirely at Pinewood was *Talk of the Devil* (1936), directed by Carol Reed. Pinewood began to lead the film industry innovation with its "unit system," enabling several films to be produced at once. It soon became the most prolific studio in the world.

As with Shepperton, the war changed the use of Pinewood as it was requisitioned by the Crown Film Unit, Army Film and Photographic Unit, RAF Film Unit and Polish Air Force Unit, which were all based there. Many classic wartime documentaries were made during this time.

Once the war ended, Pinewood was once again in production, and it was shortly to produce two landmark productions: David Lean's *Oliver Twist* (1948) and Michael Powell's *The Red Shoes* (1948), the latter noted for its use of color.

In 1971, Alfred Hitchcock was in the studio to direct his last film in Britain, the disturbing horror flick, *Frenzy*. The 1970s also saw Kevin Francis (son of Freddie Francis) set up his horror film company, Tyburn Productions, at Pinewood. With Peter Cushing as his star, he would produce *Legend of the Werewolf* and *The Ghoul* (1974), which used Heatherden Hall as a location.

In February 2000, Pinewood Studios was purchased from Rank by a management team led by Michael Grade (former Channel 4 boss) and Ivan Dunleavy. Pinewood then purchased Shepperton Studios the year after and they are now managed as one operation. Together the studios have been responsible for almost 1500 movies in their 70-year-plus existence.

SHEPPERTON STUDIOS
Studios Road, Shepperton, Middlesex
Written by Sally-Anne Ryan

Films: *And Now the Screaming Starts!* (1972), *Asylum* (1972), *The Beast Must Die* (1973), *The Black Torment* (1964), *Blind Terror* (1971), *Craze* (1974), *The Creeping Flesh* (1972), *Crucible of Terror* (1971), *Die Monster Die!* (1965), *Dr. Terror's House of Horrors* (1965), *Dracula* (1979), *The Elephant Man* (1980), *From Beyond the Grave* (1972), *Funny Man* (1994), *The House in Nightmare Park* (1972), *The House That Dripped Blood* (1970), *The Hunger* (1983), *The Innocents* (1961), *The Omen* (1976), *A Study in Terror* (1965), *Tales from the Crypt* (1972), *10 Rillington Place* (1970), *The Tomb of Ligeia* (1964), *Witchcraft* (1964)

Shepperton Studios started life as a stately home, Littleton Park, which was set in 60 acres of grounds including a stretch of the River Ash at Shepperton. These surroundings were the ideal place for its new owner, Norman Loudon, to set to work at creating one of the world's leading studios.

Loudon was a Scottish businessman who was new to the film industry. He had ambition and Littleton Park seemed like the ideal place to make his mark in this new area. This he achieved with his new company, Sound City Film Producing and Recording Studios, which he founded in 1932. By the end of that year he had successfully produced both short and feature films.

The demand for his facilities meant that in 1936 the studios were closed to enable expansion. When they re-opened, there were seven sound stages, three viewing theatres and twelve cutting rooms, alongside scene docks and workshops. Shepperton Studios were firmly on the map as the place to make movies.

During World War II, Shepperton as it was now known was used by the war office. However, close by, the Vickers-Armstrong aircraft factory was producing Spitfires and Wellington bombers, making itself a prime target for the German air raids. Stray bombs would land in the studio grounds and filming would constantly be interrupted. After a nearby factory was hit, the Ministry of Defense requisitioned the studios and put their craftsmen to work making aircraft replicas to be used in the Middle East as decoys.

The studios re-opened in 1945, and within 12 months, Norman Loudon retired from the film industry. Financial issues dominated this period, with the studio being acquired by British Lion under the leadership of Alexander Korda, the owner of London Film Productions. Korda produced and directed *An Ideal Husband* in 1947, and it was during this time that he obtained a loan of £3,000,000 to enable him to produce more films. Unfortunately, British Lion incurred high losses in the 1950s and a receiver was appointed. British Lion Films Limited was formed to take over the assets of its insolvent predecessor. This newly formed company provided distribution and financial guarantees for independent producers.

The 1950s and '60s were an extremely prolific time for the studio. Films such as *The Constant Husband* (1955), *Private's Progress* (1956), *Blue Murder at St. Trinians* (1957), *Room at the Top* (1958), *The L-Shaped Room* (1962), and *A Kind of Loving* (1962) were all produced at Shepperton.

In the 1960s and '70s the studio would become the home base of Amicus Productions, founded by Milton Subotsky and Max J. Rosenberg. These two men would be responsible for producing several classic chillers at Shepperton, including *The House That Dripped Blood, Tales from the Crypt* and *Asylum*, all of which featured Peter Cushing.

In 1984 Lee International paid £3.6 million for the studios and invested a considerable amount of money to refurbish. The '80s and '90s produced successful films such as *The Elephant Man* (1980) and *The Crying Game* (1992).

Tony and Ridley Scott acquired the studios in 1995. In 2001 Pinewood Studios bought Shepperton to enable the two companies to attract bigger-budget filmmakers.

TWICKENHAM FILM STUDIOS
St. Margaret's, Twickenham, Middlesex
Written by Brian Holland

Films: *An American Werewolf in London* (1981), *The Night Digger* (1971), *Repulsion* (1965), *Straw Dogs* (1971), *Vault of Horror* (1973)

The Twickenham site was bought in 1912 by Dr. Ralph Jupp, who formed the London Film Company to produce stylish films for the American market, his first being *The House of Temperley* in 1913. Later came *Masks and Faces* (1917), which was made to raise funds for the Royal Academy of Dramatic Art (RADA), and boasted on-screen cameos from George Bernard Shaw and J.M. Barrie. In 1920, Financial and health problems caused Jupp to sell to the Alliance Company, but this only lasted a matter of two years.

From 1923 to 1926 the studios were leased to various companies. In 1927, the British government responded to concerns of an American-based monopoly on motion pictures with the Cinematographic Film Act, which decreed that twenty percent of all films shown in Britain would be produced there. One of the first to take advantage of the immediate surge of filmmaking was the Hamburg-born film producer Julius Hagen, who secured the lease of the studio and named it Twickenham Film Studios. Under this name the studio continues to the present day.

During World War II, filming was discontinued due to bomb damage. The studio struggled to recapture its former success throughout the 1950s, focusing primarily on early television productions. The turning point came with the appointment of Guido Coen as executive director in 1959. Coen developed the studio's international profile, beginning with the hard-hitting drama *Saturday Night, Sunday Morning* (1960), starring Albert Finney and Rachel Roberts. Under his guidance, Twickenham Film Studios would reach its peak in the 1960s. One of the films attracting most attention was *A Hard Day's Night*, directed in 1964 by Richard Lester, and starring The Beatles.

Many other acclaimed films have been made at the studio, or have used its post-production facilities. They include *Zulu* (1964), *Superman II* (1981), *Gandhi* (1982), *Blade Runner* (1982), and *A Fish Called Wanda* (1988).

In 1971 Sam Peckinpah made his violent and horrific film *Straw Dogs* at Twickenham, and in 1981 John Landis filmed his hugely successful horror comedy *An American Werewolf in London* at the studio.

Today, although the work at Twickenham Film Studios is centered on television programs and commercials, there is a continuing film presence, with directors and producers relying upon the studio's state-of-the-art facilities to complete their motion pictures.

Locations — In Detail

Aldenham : Hertfordshire

Films: *Dracula A.D. 1972* (1971), *Fear in the Night* (1971), *Village of the Damned* (1960)

The parish of Aldenham, which contains the minute village of Aldenham and the village of Letchmore Heath, has a population of about 3,000.

Aldenham certainly dates from Saxon times and it is believed that the chancel of the church of St. John the Baptist (*Village of the Damned*) is the site of a Saxon church built by Offa, king of Mercia (785 AD). In the Treasury of Westminster Abbey is a charter (the earliest they possess) in which lands were granted at Aldenham in return for the present of a gold armlet.

The Domesday Book of 1086 has this entry with regard to Aldenham: "Eldeham: Westminster Abbey before and after 1066: Geoffrey de Bec from St. Albans church."

The village of Letchmore Heath (*Village of the Damned*) is not listed in the Domesday Book and the first reference to any of its inhabitants was in the sixteenth century. But the name Letchmore originates from Anglo Saxon words "Leche mere," meaning "dirty pond." The pond is still there and a very beautiful feature of the village — but it is not dirty!

The parish of Aldenham is a "green lung" preserved by being in the Green Belt, and Aldenham and Letchmore Heath are both conservation areas. A country park has been constructed at Aldenham Old Reservoir and a nature reserve at the New Reservoir. The parish is much visited in the summer by tourists who may wish to visit the country and Letchmore Heath with its seventeenth century inn, picturesque village green and pond, and its many sixteenth century cottages. Aldenham is also a popular place for fishermen who frequently go fishing at the Tykes Water Lake (*Dracula A.D. 1972*).

The twelfth century Aldenham church (St. John the Baptist) is a beautiful building, with many brasses and tombs, with a fine peal of bells. The church is unique as its tower and tower buttresses have been built using Hertfordshire puddingstone, a very rare geological rock found only around the area of Aldenham and Radlett.

The inhabitants of the parish have changed dramatically in the last 80 years. In 1920 Letchmore Heath was an isolated village which the residents rarely had to leave, as all that was necessary was available within the village itself. There were three pubs, two village stores (one with a post office), a bakery, a butchershop, an undertaking establishment, a haberdashery and two tailorshops.

There was also a village school and two chapels. Ninety percent of the residents worked on the local farm, at Aldenham House (*Village of the Damned*) or at the school.

Today the two villages have become the home of many commuters who leave daily to work in either London or Watford.

Aldenham is also home to the Krishna consciousness religious sect, who are based at Bhaktivedanta Manor (*Fear in the Night*) in Letchmore Heath.

Alnwick Castle : Alnwick, Northumberland*

Film: *Count Dracula* (1977)

The market town of Alnwick is one of Northumberland's most attractive. It sits on the gently rising ground overlooking the valley of the River Aln, the town being dominated by the huge castle belonging to the Dukes of Northumberland. It is of such importance that the town is sometimes called the "Windsor of the North"; Alnwick Castle is the second largest inhabited castle in Britain, being the home of the Percys, earls and dukes of Northumberland since 1309. The earliest mention of Alnwick Castle in the history books appears soon after 1096 when Yves de Vescy became baron of Alnwick and erected the earliest parts of the castle.

The castle was first restored by the first Lord Percy of Alnwick in the early 1300s; portions of this restoration remain today, including the Abbot's Tower, the Middle Gateway and the Constable's Tower. In the sixteenth and seventeenth centuries the earls of Northumberland ceased to live in the castle, and it fell into disrepair. However, Algernon, seventh Duke of Somerset, one of the descendents of the earls of Northumberland, whose line died out in 1670, returned to Alnwick Castle in the early eighteenth century. He was the first family member to live there in over a century. In the mid–eighteenth century his son, the first duke of Northumberland began a major project to restore the castle. The famous architect, Robert Adam, was employed, and the castle was developed in a Gothic style. Many new windows were added and stone statues placed on the outside of the building. In the eighteenth and nineteenth cen-

---

*www.alnwickcastle.com. Written by Brian Holland.

turies the parks and gardens surrounding the castle were also developed and were landscaped to make them more ornamental.

It is not surprising that such an imposing structure should have been chosen to feature in many famous films over the years: *Becket*, starring Richard Burton and Peter O'Toole, in 1964, *Robin Hood: Prince of Thieves*, starring Kevin Costner, in 1991, and of course the *Harry Potter* movies (as Hogwarts School).

Its Gothic style was used to great effect when it doubled as Castle Dracula in the 1977 BBC version of the Bram Stoker classic starring Louis Jourdan as the count.

Today, Alnwick Castle is home to the duke and duchess of Northumberland, who open its doors to the public in the spring and summer.

Blenheim Palace : Woodstock, Oxfordshire*

Film: *Frankenstein: The True Story* (1973), *The Legend of Hell House* (1973)

Doubling as the splendid interior of the Fanshawe house in *Frankenstein: The True Story*, and also featured as the meeting place between Dr. Barrett and Mr. Deutsch at the opening of *The Legend of Hell House*, Blenheim is a beautiful architectural masterpiece.

The name Blenheim comes from a decisive battle that took place on August 13, 1704, on the north bank of the river Danube, near a small village called Blindheim or Blenheim. It was here that the first duke of Marlborough, John Churchill, won a great victory for the allies over the forces of Louis XIV, thus saving Europe from French domination.

As a reward for defending Holland and Austria from invasion by the French, Queen Anne granted Marlborough the Royal Manor of Woodstock and told him that she would build him a house, at her own expense, which would be called Blenheim.

Building began in 1705. There is an inscription on the East Gate giving details, including the fact that £240,000 was given as a grant towards the cost of the build.

While abroad, others plotted against Marlborough's favor with the queen and the result was that on his return he found that the promised money wasn't forthcoming and some £45,000 was still outstanding to the architect, Sir J. Vanbrugh, and others who had undertaken the project. In the summer of 1712 all work on Blenheim Palace had to stop because of the lack of funds. However, following the death of Queen Anne in 1714, the duke and duchess of Marlborough negotiated with the unpaid artisans and suppliers and the palace was completed at their own expense.

It was at Blenheim Palace that at 1:30 A.M. on November 30, 1874,

*www.blenheimpalace.com. Written by Brian Holland.

The Legend of Hell House: Blenheim Palace, Woodstock, Oxfordshire, features at the opening of the film (the meeting between Dr. Barrett and Mr. Deutsch). (Photograph by the author.)

Winston Churchill, the "greatest Briton of all time," was born. Typical of the impatience that he was to demonstrate in later life, he arrived several weeks early.

It was also in the gardens of Blenheim, at the Temple of Diana, that Churchill proposed to Clementine Hozier during the summer of 1908.

Churchill's love of Blenheim remained to his dying day. At his request, when he passed away in 1965, he was buried beside his parents, Lord and Lady Randolph Churchill, in the nearby churchyard at Bladon. When Lady Clementine Churchill died in 1977, her remains were laid to rest beside those of her husband.

Brocket Hall : Welwyn, Hertfordshire*

Films: *Night of the Demon* (1957), *Omen III—The Final Conflict* (1981)

When it comes to a rich and varied history, Brocket Hall has one of the most intriguing of any of the great houses of Britain.

*www.brocket-hall.co.uk.

It was built by renowned architect, James Paine, for the owner, Sir Mathew Lamb, in 1760. The Hall stands on the site of two predecessors, the original of which was built in 1239.

Sir Mathew's son would become the Hall's first Lord Melbourne. His wife was the mistress of the flamboyant Prince Regent, later to be crowned George IV. He was a frequent visitor to the Hall and created the Chinese suite of rooms (known as the Prince Regent suite) which is still used by guests today.

Romantic liaisons were abundant at Brocket Hall, with the wife of the second Lord Melbourne, Lady Caroline Lamb, having a passion for the poet, Lord Byron. The relationship was stormy and it is said that she fell swooning from her horse at the shock of seeing Byron's funeral cortege near to the Brocket estate (she had not known until then that he had died!).

The second Lord Melbourne eventually became prime minister and formed a close friendship with Queen Victoria, who often visited the Hall and came to regard Melbourne as her mentor.

On his death in 1848, Brocket Hall was passed to his sister, who would marry Lord Palmerston. He too became prime minister and was to die in somewhat bizarre circumstances at Brocket Hall involving a chambermaid.

Every beautiful country hall must also have a sinister side, and Brocket is no exception: It housed the child of Satan, Damien Thorn (Sam Neill), planning his next murderous act in *Omen III—The Final Conflict*, and occultist Karswell (Niall MacGinnis), raising a giant medieval devil to dispose of his enemies in the classic horror *Night of the Demon*.

Today Brocket Hall is a hotel, offering visitors a warm welcome into one of England's great stately homes. It retains its famous collection of paintings and fine furniture, much of which was made for the house.

Camelot Castle : Tintagel, Cornwall*

Film: *Dracula* (1979)

With all the legendary lore which cluster round the ruined castle of King Arthur, picturesquely perched on the crest of a rocky promontory, rising precipitously from the sea, Tintagel, Cornwall, offers attractions to the tourist beyond even the beauty of its rugged cliff scenery, and the salubrity of its bracing air coming in straight from the open Atlantic.

Situated on high ground, overlooking the old castle ruins, a handsome hotel, appropriately named King Arthur's Castle, is reared up on the sea front. It is a massive and imposing block of buildings in castellated style of architectural and forms a prominent object on the landscape. It played the Seward Institute in John Badham's lavish screen production of *Dracula*. Frank Langella

*www.camelotcastle.com

(Dracula) watched his prey from the battlements, and Van Helsing (Laurence Olivier) and Dr. Seward (Donald Pleasence) disposed of vampiric Lucy (Jan Francis) afore the Castle, looking out over a misty sea.

King Arthur's Castle Hotel was built in 1894 by a company formed by Sir Robert Harvey. It opened at Easter 1899, after taking five years to complete. Harvey later purchased the hotel outright, and upon his death it was handed down to his son.

The property stood empty for two years, until it was purchased by Letty Rundle in March 1953. She immediately set about the interior décor and refurnished the ground floor and first floor bedrooms, which were opened in June 1953. Two years later, the second and third floor was completed.

In the early sixties she brought her son Patrick and daughter Rosemarie into the partnership as co-owners. After 50 years of ownership, they passed the hotel over to the present-day proprietors, Mr. and Mrs. John Mappin and Mr. Ted Stourton, because of their love of natural beauty, mythology and art.

Camelot Castle faces one of Britain's most stunning views, and welcomes visitors to see it for themselves. While you're about it, why not book room 117 — the room Laurence Olivier used while filming *Dracula*. His signed photograph hangs over the mantelpiece.

Castle Acre Priory : Castle Acre, Nr. Swaffham, Norfolk

Film: *The Tomb of Ligeia* (1964)

As home to brooding eccentric Verden Fell (Vincent Price) in Roger Corman's cult Victorian horror movie *The Tomb of Ligeia*, the priory at Castle Acre was inspired by the Abbey of Cluny in Burgundy, and actually home to a community of monks until 1537, when Henry VIII disbanded all monastic houses.

The edifice dates back to 1090. Among the ruined walls and towers of this extensive site are a beautiful church, with an elaborately decorated front; a gatehouse; a private chapel; and prior's lodgings, which are actually still fit to live in. Despite several alterations and extensions to the original building, the prior's lodgings and his chapel are impressive, and many medieval features remain in the converted dwelling house.

The whole structure presents an image of contrasts: There's such splendid detail and completeness in some of the buildings, yet much of the ruined site is almost unrecognizable. There's a distinct "monastic" presence, yet the apparent opulence is more in keeping with a grand old manor house.

Open to the public, it provides a perfect setting for the visitor seeking a place of calm and serenity, a welcome temporary refuge from today's fast-moving world.

The Tomb of Ligeia: Castle Acre Priory, Castle Acre, Nr. Swaffham, Norfolk, doubles as the home to brooding eccentric Verden Fell (Vincent Price) in this Roger Corman cult classic. (Photograph by the author.)

Chislehurst Caves : Old Hill, Chislehurst, Kent*

Film: *Inseminoid* (1980)

Chislehurst Caves are a labyrinth of dark, mysterious passageways, an ideal setting for an underground space headquarters as featured in the alien horror *Inseminoid*, in which Judy Geeson isn't quite what she seems.

The caves themselves have been hewn by hand from the chalk, deep beneath Chislehurst. There are over 20 miles of caverns and passageways, dug over a period of 8000 years. The vast complex of caves is a maze of ancient mines originally carved out in the search for flint and chalk. They are actually divided into three main sections, Saxon, Druid and Roman. Each section was later connected by digging joining passages.

The presence of chalk has been important to civilizations over thousands of years, and still is to date. Mining chalk provides lime and flint.

Lime is the basic for plaster and whitewash paint, and flint was used for manufacturing tools by early man and later for building. The mining activity is difficult to date; however, the mines do appear on a charter circa 1250 and also in local church records of 1737.

*www.chislehurstcaves.co.uk

The last time the mines were known to have been worked was around the 1830s when the Saxon section was used by a flintmaker and limeburner. The local railway made the mines more accessible in 1865, and this helped make it a tourist attraction. The caves also became the setting for several underground concerts in the early 1900s.

During World War II the caves were turned into a massive air raid shelter because of constant bombings over London. There is even a chapel. One child was born in the caves during World War II, and she was given the name Cavina.

The caves in recent years have been used as a venue for live music, with Jimi Hendrix, The Who, The Beatles and Pink Floyd all having played there.

It is said that the caves are haunted, and that Druids once made grisly human sacrifices in their depths. Today, however, the caves are a major tourist attraction, open to the public most days throughout the year.

Cliveden House Hotel : Taplow, Buckinghamshire*

Film: *Frankenstein: The True Story* (1973)

Cliveden House Hotel in Taplow, on the Buckinghamshire Berkshire border, is remarkable in that it is the only stately home in the UK which is also a hotel — and a luxurious one at that, with five red stars and placed firmly in the upper echelons of the AA's Top 200 Hotels in the UK and Ireland.

It is set in 376 acres of beautiful grounds and gardens amidst the rolling Buckinghamshire countryside. The house itself stands upon a dramatic chalk cliff offering breathtaking views of Berkshire and the River Thames.

The first house was actually built in 1666 by the second duke of Buckingham, who was well known as a notorious rake, schemer and wit; it is said that he created Cliveden as a hunting lodge where he could entertain his various friends, along with his mistress. Since then it has twice been destroyed by fire, only to emerge, phoenix-like and more stunning than before. The house also has the distinction of having played host to virtually every British monarch since George I and has been home to three dukes, an earl and Frederick, prince of Wales.

Queen Victoria, a frequent guest at Cliveden, was reportedly not amused when in 1893 the house was bought by William Waldorf Astor, America's richest citizen. Aston subsequently gave the estate to his son and daughter-in-law in 1906 and thereafter it became the hub of a hectic social whirl. Guests included everyone from Charlie Chaplin to Winston Churchill, and President Roosevelt to George Bernard Shaw.

Harold Macmillan, another frequent guest, was told that the house was

---

*www.clivedenhousehotel.co.uk. Written by Brian Holland.

eventually to become a hotel and remarked, "My dear boy, it always has been." The tradition of impeccable hospitality and extravagant entertainment continues to this day and makes a stay at Cliveden the experience of a lifetime.

This most glamorous and starry of houses has featured in many films, including *Carrington* (1995), starring Emma Thompson; *Carry On — Don't Lose Your Head* (1966), starring Sid James and the Carry On team; Lord Attenborough's *Chaplin* (1992), starring Robert Downey Jr., and *Thunderbirds* (2003), where the hotel was Lady Penelope's house.

It also appeared in the all-star three-hour horror production, *Frankenstein: The True Story*, doubling as the lavish country home of the Fanshawes.

Culzean Castle : Maybole, South Ayrshire, Scotland

Film: *The Wicker Man* (1973)

Overlooking the sea, with views to the Isle of Arran and the Mull of Kintyre, stands the beautiful Culzean Castle. Its appearance today is a far cry from its origins as an L-shaped tower house of the 1590s built by Sir Thomas Kennedy. The Kennedys claimed descent from the Earls of Carrick and thus a relationship with Robert Bruce. At one time an important family in the Scottish royal circle, the Kennedys like the Bruces before them had a varied and sometimes murky history.

After the eighth earl died without an heir, and a protracted legal dispute about the succession, the title was granted to Sir Thomas Kennedy of Culzean in 1762. He decided to improve and modernize the castle. He was followed by his brother, David, who inherited in 1775. David employed a renowned architect of the time for this new building.

The building took place in four phases between 1777 and 1792, incorporating some of the original sixteenth century stonework. The architect, Robert Adam, carried out an incredible scheme of enlargement and decoration in Neoclassical style. The ceilings, plasterwork moldings and paintings (by Antonio Zucchi), together with the color schemes, all reflect this.

There are also many original elements from Adam's time, including Chippendale, Hepplewhite and Sheraton furniture. The rooms provide a wonderfully elegant contrast to the wild seascape outside, with the circular saloon and oval staircase being particular highlights.

The estate was given to the National Trust of Scotland in 1945 and considerable restoration and conservation was done both inside and outside the castle.

It was also instructed that part of the castle be given to General Eisenhower, for his lifetime, as a thank you from Scotland for commanding Scottish soldiers in the battle of Europe.

Eisenhower visited Culzean four times, once as president, and then during his retirement. He enjoyed golfing, painting and walking in the peace and quiet of Culzean's beautiful gardens, woodland and seashore. "This is a place where I can relax," he wrote. An exhibition in the castle tells something of Eisenhower's achievements and of his visits to Culzean.

Today, thanks to the National Trust of Scotland and Scottish Heritage USA, the grounds have been opened as a country park and the castle is used as a venue for weddings and various functions. Eisenhower's holiday home now provides beautiful accommodations in six double bedrooms, making it perhaps the most exclusive place to stay anywhere in Scotland.

It has also had its fame as a film location, providing the perfect setting for the home of Lord Summerisle (Christopher Lee), the evil leader of a strange and sinister cult, in *The Wicker Man.*

Edgwarebury Corus Hotel : Barnet Lane, Elstree, Borehamwood, Hertfordshire

Film: *The Devil Rides Out* (1968)

As you walk through the front door at Edgwarebury, which was originally part of the dungeons in Lewes Castle, Sussex, your attention is immediately drawn to the outstanding features of the fireplace with Italian carved columns supporting the ornate mantelpiece.

The decorative frieze paintings around the upper part of the reception lobby (executed by Sir Norman Little) depict scenes from the Spanish Armada. Some of the wood was actually from ships involved in this battle.

The wooden panels in the Beaufort Room are believed to date back to the 1600s. In the bar, there is a fine set of old Gothic panels made from ships lockers. The fireplace overmantel features some carving which frames a medieval Spanish painting produced on a leather "canvas."

The Edgwarebury is set in ten acres of garden and natural woodland, with views overlooking central London. Some of the gardens shrubs and rhododendrons are of the same age as the house itself, which dates back to 1540.

The Tudor house was transformed into a hotel in the late 1960s. Recent expansion (1989) added conference rooms which moved the hotel to its present status.

Over the years many television productions and films have featured the Edgwarebury, including the Hammer horror classic *The Devil Rides Out,* in which the Duke de Richleau (Christopher Lee) performs a ritual at Edgwarebury to save Simon (Patrick Mower) from losing his soul to the forces of darkness.

In addition to this "claim to fame," the Edgwarebury can boast of having entertained many famous celebrities, including Peter Sellers, Tom Cruise, John Cleese and Stanley Kubrick.

Ettington Park Hotel : Alderminster, Stratford-upon-Avon, Warwickshire

Films: *The Haunting* (1963), *The Watcher in the Woods* (1980)

No place in England has been associated with one family longer than Ettington Park. The first record of the Shirley family at Ettington appeared in the Domesday Book over 900 years ago, and it is possible that they lived here before the Norman Conquest.

The house's rich and colorful history is written all over it. You'll see it in the scores of friezes, stained glass windows, chimneypieces, carved panels and coats of arms that embellish its walls. For instance, the frieze which appears over a bay window, depicting a page bringing a Saracen's head to Sir Thomas Shirley in the Holy Land.

Throughout the house's history, members of the Shirley family have left their mark. In 1820, John Shirley rebuilt the library and copied the chimneypiece so as to look like one from Windsor Castle. His son, Evelyn Philip Shirley, left his own lasting monument when he rebuilt the house in high gothic style between 1858 and 1862.

This spectacular neo–Gothic mansion has been used to good effect in two classic movies.

The Haunting, filmed at Ettington in 1963, is certainly one of the most chilling specter movies of all time. Much of the film's shocking power comes from the somewhat eerie appearance of Ettington, beautifully captured by cinematographer David Boulton.

In the Walt Disney–produced film *The Watcher in the Woods* starring Bette Davis, Ettington is the home of sinister recluse Ian Bannen, holding onto a dark secret from his childhood.

Throughout its history, though, Ettington is far from eerie. It's a warm and much loved home, built for pleasure. And now, as a hotel, its quiet opulence and beautiful surroundings provide the ideal place for you to relax and indulge yourself—just as guests in the past must have done. But do beware: It is said to be the most haunted hotel in Britain.

Fountains Abbey : Ripon, North Yorkshire*

Film: *Omen III—The Final Conflict* (1981)

A dispute and riot at St. Mary's Abbey in York led to the founding of Fountains Abbey in 1132. After pleading unsuccessfully to return to the early sixth century rule of St. Benedict, 13 monks were exiled and taken into the

*www.fountainsabbey.org.uk

protection of Thurstan, Archbishop of York. He provided them with a site in the valley of the little River Skell. Although described as a place "more fit for wild beasts than men to inhabit," it had all the essential materials for the creation of a monastery: shelter from the weather, stone and timber for building, and plenty of water.

Three years later the exiled monks became part of the Cistercian Order, founded in France in 1098. Under its rule they lived a rigorous daily life, were committed to long periods of silence, followed a diet barely above subsistence level, and wore the regulation habit of coarse undyed sheep's wool (underwear was forbidden), which earned them the name White Monks.

One of the Abbey's most important developments was the introduction of the Cistercian system of lay brothers. They were usually illiterate and relieved the monks from routine jobs. Many served as Masons, tanners, shoemakers and smiths, but their chief role was to look after the Abbey's vast flocks of sheep, which lived in the huge estate stretching westwards from Fountains to the Lake District.

Without the lay brothers, Fountains could never have attained its great wealth or economic importance. By the middle of the thirteenth century it was one of England's richest religious houses. In addition to farming, they mined lead, worked iron, quarryied stones and bred horses.

In the fourteenth century, economic collapse followed bad harvests, and the Black Death exacerbated the situation.

Despite its problems, Fountains Abbey remained of considerable importance in the Cistercian Order, and for a short time it did flourish again, but its life was brought to an abrupt end in 1539 by Henry VIII's Dissolution of Monasteries. After passing through several hands it slowly decayed into what it is today — a ruin — which is open to members of the public on a daily basis.

This ruin features at the climax of, *Omen III—The Final Conflict*, in which the Antichrist Damien Thorn (Sam Neill) is finally brought to his death by Christ.

Grim's Dyke Hotel : Old Redding, Harrow Weald, London*

Films: *Blood Beast Terror* (1968), *Cry of the Banshee* (1970), *The Curse of the Crimson Altar* (1968), *Endless Night* (1971), *Haunted House of Horror* (1969)

As Inspector Quennell (Peter Cushing) checks out a bloody corpse at the entrance of the house in *Blood Beast Terror*, and Vincent Price as Lord Whitman gets up to his usual nasty tricks from within in *Cry of the Banshee*, we can safely say that Grim's Dyke has played host to some famous faces — not least,

*www.grimsdyke.com

the master of horror himself, Boris Karloff, trying to stop demonic Christopher Lee from turning the house into a den of witchcraft in *The Curse of the Crimson Altar*.

Grim's Dyke is also associated with another famous name, that of Sir William Schwenck Gilbert, the writing half of the Gilbert & Sullivan partnership. He lived in the house from 1890 until his death in 1911.

The house was built in 1870 for the Victorian painter Frederick Goodall, and completed by 1872. It was designed by Norman Shaw, a well-known architect of the time who also designed the New Scotland Yard building.

The Gilberts bought the property in 1890, and Sir William's greatest joy was the large lake he had excavated to the south of the house. Every day in the summer he would bathe there — a habit which eventually cost him his life. On May 29, 1911, he invited two local girls to swim in the lake. He died attempting to help one of them when she got into difficulties.

Gilbert seems to have lived very happily at Grim's Dyke though, and worked every day in the library where he could look out through the French windows onto the croquet lawn. He invited many of his friends, including Bram Stoker, to stay at the house.

After her husband's passing, Lady Gilbert remained in the house, surrounded by their many animals and pets, until her death in 1936.

During the years that followed, it became a frequent television and film location. It was invaded by Daleks for the 1966 *Doctor Who* adventure *The Evil of the Daleks*.

In 1970, Grim's Dyke was converted into a hotel and designated a building of special architectural and historical interest. A far cry from doubling as a haunted old manor in the fright flicks *Haunted House of Horror* and *Endless Night*.

The present owners took over in 1996 when the Grade II–listed building was extensively restored and refurbished in the country house style. In its interior, you will find good food, fine wines and courteous service.

So go on, give it a try. You never know who you might bump into. Perhaps old Boris!

Harlaxton Manor : Harlaxton, Grantham, Lincolnshire

Film: *The Haunting* (1999)

No manor house could be more striking, more beautifully Gothic than Harlaxton, built in the 1830s for Gregory Gregory, a wealthy Nottinghamshire businessman, to replace the original Elizabethan manor house in Harlaxton village.

Having travelled throughout England and Europe seeking inspiration, ideas and artifacts for this huge house, Gregory employed Anthony Salvin, a well-known country house architect. Harlaxton must be regarded as Salvin's masterpiece. Built with the exuberant merging of Gothic, Jacobethan and Baroque styles, it has an unforgettable and dramatic impact.

Is it any wonder that this masterpiece would play the part of Hill House in the remake of *The Haunting*? In this 1999 release, Lili Taylor, Liam Neeson and Catherine Zeta-Jones are stalked by the many specters hiding within its grand walls of sculptures and ghostly faces.

Few houses in the English countryside can match the splendid approach to Harlaxton. A straight mile-long drive leads under the gatehouse to Salvin's towering façade. Whether by day or night it is a memorable experience.

The Haunting (1999): Doubling as Hill House is the beautifully gothic Harlaxton Manor, Harlaxton, Grantham, Lincolnshire. (Photograph by the author.)

The house is presently in the ownership of the University of Evansville, Indiana, and is used as that U.S. institution's British campus.

The Hermit's Chapel : Roche Rock, Roche, Cornwall*

Film: *Omen III—The Final Conflict* (1981)

The ruins perched on top of Roche Rock are those of a fifteenth century chapel and hermitage, where legend tells that St. Gonand — one of Cornwall's lesser-known saints — tended to her father, a leper.

It is said that the chapel was built in 1409. Today a dangerous winding track over broken rocks leads up to the remains of the tiny chapel, where a steel ladder is attached to the rock outcrop, leading up to the top. If you are game for a climb, try it — but take care.

It was here in *Omen III—The Final Conflict* that Brother Matteus meets his doom, as members of his own brethren stab him to death, mistaking him for Antichrist, Damien Thorn.

*Written by Brian Holland.

The chapel is associated with the legends of both King Arthur and Jan Tregeagle, an unpopular seventeenth century Cornish magistrate. Some Arthurian scholars suggest that this was one of the hiding places of Tristan and Iseult, the doomed lovers who were continually fleeing from King Mark, and that it was from here that Tristan threw himself to his death from the chapel window as the king's men approached. Unable to live without her love, Iseult followed shortly after.

Legend says that Tregeagle made a great fortune through dubious deals and swindles, but spent half of his money bribing the local clergy to bury him in consecrated ground after his death. This they did, but he was later summoned back from the dead to appear as a witness in a court case about some disputed land. Having been thus summoned, Tregeagle was himself then found guilty of fraud by the court, being set a series of tasks that would keep him occupied for all eternity, but so long as he worked then he would be spared from the Devil. He was given the task of emptying a bottomless pool with only a cracked limpet shell. A pack of vicious hounds were set to guard him, ready to attack if he stopped work, for even a second.

One night during a fierce storm he stopped work and managed to run across Bodmin Moor towards the chapel, the hounds in hot pursuit. When he reached the chapel he only managed to thrust his head through the window before getting stuck, and his body was left for the hounds to devour. His screams were so loud that eventually one of the clergy came to his rescue, freed Tregeagle and banished him forever to the moors.

Legend says that the ghost of Tregeagle can now be seen wandering on Bodmin Moor and around the chapel, performing endless tasks and mournfully wailing over his misfortune.

Highgate Cemetery : Swain's Lane, London*

Films: *Frankenstein and the Monster from Hell* (1972), *From Beyond the Grave* (1972), *Tales from the Crypt* (1972), *Taste the Blood of Dracula* (1969)

On the land on which Highgate Cemetery is located, previously stood the manor and estate of Sir William Ashurst, lord mayor of London (1693–94) and director of the Bank of England. Sir William died in 1720 and by the beginning of the nineteenth century the estate had fallen into disrepair.

In 1836 the newly formed London Cemetery Company secured the land for development. After three years' construction, Highgate opened its gates in 1839. Immediately it became something of a tourist attraction due to its fine Romantic-Gothic architecture and Egyptian-style catacombs.

With the legislation of cremation in 1888, however, the cemetery's profits

*www.Highgate-cemetery.org.

slowly declined, and by the 1950s the gardeners who tended to the many geometric ornamental flower beds were one by one released from its employment, leaving nature to gradually reclaim the ground. By the late 1960s the cemetery was overgrown, vandalized, and running at a loss.

During this period a number of film companies exploited and immortalized its beauty on celluloid. Amongst them were Amicus and Hammer, who would bring a heavy and very effective shroud of mist to Highgate. In *Taste the Blood of Dracula* (1969) the resurrected figure of Count Dracula (Christopher Lee) conducts his lair of vampires from deep within the cemeteries, and in *Frankenstein and the Monster from Hell* (1972) a hapless gravedigger (Patrick Troughton) is caught by the law (Norman Mitchell) for digging up corpses and handing them over to scientist (Shane Briant). It has been put to equally good use for the creepy opening credits of both *Tales from the Crypt* (1972) and *From Beyond the Grave* (1972).

By 1975 the cemetery itself had ceased to be financially viable, and so the owners, United Cemeteries, had the imposing cast iron gates locked, and it was closed down. The main buildings had become dilapidated and the landscape choked with brambles and self-sown sycamores.

It was at this time that the Highgate Society formed The Friends of Highgate, and through generous financial support and with the help of volunteers, they were able to bring the cemetery back to its former glory.

Today, tours are given around this beautiful piece of historical and English architecture. You can see the strange circle of vaults, the Egyptian avenue, the terraced catacombs and mausoleums all now painstakingly restored. The tour guide also tells you about some of the 850 notable people buried at Highgate, among them Karl Marx, George Eliot and Sir Ralph Richardson.

But whatever you do, if you take that tour — don't mention the horror films!

Kentwell Hall : Long Melford, Suffolk*

Film: *Witchfinder General* (1968)

Kentwell Hall is a moated, redbrick Tudor manor house, built for the Clopton family in the 1600s with wealth created in the wool trade.

The exterior of the house has changed little in 450 years. The interior was remodeled slightly in 1825, with the present owners enhancing that restoration.

Emphasizing their Tudor origins are the great hall and dining room, while the library and the drawing room are classical in style.

Kentwell still remains a family home, and the owners, Patrick and Judith Phillips, are enthusiastic in their restoration of the house, which has included

*www.kentwellhall.co.uk.

essential structural repairs and the replacement of a Georgian sash window with leaded lights.

The hall is also home to the Recreations of Tudor Domestic Life which is held for two weeks in the summer and on holiday weekends. Volunteers wear Tudor costumes and recreate life as it would have been at Kentwell Hall for the gentry, their visitors and servants, with the great kitchen, dairy, bakery and forge fully equipped in the original sixteenth century manner.

Approaching the house is a magnificent avenue of lime trees, which is surrounded by extensive grounds. There are clipped yews, a fine herb garden and a walled garden with a seventeenth century manner.

The hall is supposedly haunted by several ghosts. There are also tales of a coachman and horses haunting its grounds.

In 1968 Kentwell became a film location as the evil Matthew Hopkins (Vincent Price) swam some of his victims in its moat to test them for witchery in the cult horror movie *Witchfinder General*.

In the summer Kentwell has open air Shakespeare and opera concerts.

Knebworth House : Knebworth, Hertfordshire*

Films: *Horror Hospital* (1973), *The Lair of the White Worm* (1988), *The Monster Club* (1980)

One of England's most beloved stately homes, Knebworth House is famous worldwide for the many rock stars who have performed within its grounds, including Pink Floyd, The Rolling Stones, Led Zeppelin and Queen.

It was built by Sir Robert Lytton in 1490, and over the next 300 years the house was greatly added to by following generations of the family.

In 1810 Mrs. Elizabeth Bulwer-Lytton had a large part of the house demolished, while her son, Sir Edward Bulwer-Lytton, the Victorian novelist and statesman (and author of the words "The pen is mightier than the sword"), transformed the house into the High Gothic palace seen today, complete with battlements, domes, turrets, griffins, stained glass and gargoyles.

The interior is designed in many styles, including a Jacobean banqueting hall, the Gothic state drawing room, the Victorian state dining room, the Tudor-style Queen Elizabeth room, and the Regency bedroom of Mrs. Bulwer-Lytton.

Designs from the twentieth century are shown in Edwin Lutyens' Entrance Hall, Dining Parlour and Library.

Knebworth House has 25 acres of gardens which were simplified by Edwin Lutyens. These include the formal rose garden, pollarded lime avenues and maze.

www.knebworthhouse.com

There is also a herb garden designed by Gertrude Jekyll. It is surrounded by 250 acres of parkland in which herds of red deer roam.

As well as being a venue for rock concerts, it has also played host to many film companies, doubling on one occasion as Dr. Storm's (Michael Gough) Health Hotel; his patients get more than they bargained for, including lobotomies in the gruesome comic chiller *Horror Hospital*. In *The Monster Club* it is home to Shadmock (James Laurenson), whom you must never double-cross. It doubled as D'Ampton Hall in the Ken Russell vampire flick *The Lair of the White Worm*. Probably its most notable film appearance was as Wayne Manor in Tim Burton's *Batman*.

A unique piece of architecture, Knebworth is open to the public, whether for historic or film interest.

Lavenham : Suffolk

Film: *Witchfinder General* (1968)

Lavenham is widely acknowledged as the best example of a medieval wool town in England.

In Tudor times, Lavenham was said to be the fourteenth wealthiest town in England, despite its small size. Its fine timber-framed buildings and beautiful church, built on the success of the wool trade, make it a fascinating place to explore today.

Although Lavenham goes back to Saxon times, it is best known as a medieval wool town. It was granted its market charter in 1257 and started exporting its famous blue broadcloth as far afield as Russia.

In the fourteenth century, Edward III encouraged the English weaving industry, and Lavenham began to prosper. However, in the late sixteenth century, Dutch refugees in Colchester began weaving a lighter, cheaper and more fashionable cloth and the woolen trade in Lavenham began to fail.

Most of the buildings in Lavenham today date from the fifteenth century and, amazingly, many of these have never been altered. Late 15th-century timber-framed Guild Hall dominates the town's market square.

In addition to its many historic buildings, Lavenham is also blessed with good pubs, fine places to eat and fascinating antique shops to browse around.

It has, unsurprisingly, regularly been a film location; in 1975 Stanley Kubrick shot some scenes for his film *Barry Lyndon* in Lavenham. For horror movie lovers, it is most famous for its appearance in Michael Reeves' powerful film *Witchfinder General*, in which Matthew Hopkins (Vincent Price) burns to death a young woman, Elizabeth Clark, in the market square. (As a note of interest, the real Hopkins actually past through Lavenham during his reign of terror in the seventeenth century.)

Littledean Jail : Littledean, Nr. Cinderford, Royal Forest of Dean, Gloucestershire*

Film: *House of Whipcord* (1974)

The dark and eerie film *House of Whipcord* was filmed on location around the Royal Forest of Dean in Gloucestershire, *House of Whipcord* fans visiting this area will instantly recognize the exterior of Littledean Jail, remaining exactly as it was when the movie was shot there in 1974. It's a spooky place indeed to walk around and see the windows where Anne-Marie (Penny Irving) looked out, trying desperately to plot her escape.

Previously a house of correction, then a local courthouse, Littledean Jail is now a museum, housing an extraordinary and vast crime collection. Exhibits range from paraphernalia of the occult and letters from serial killers, to Saddam Hussein's toilet seat. The exterior remains in excellent condition and inside you can see the cells as they were when the building was built in 1882.

Many infamous characters and rogues were said to have been tried and held here. Local character Fred West was charged at this court in his petty criminal days, and later became world-renowned for the 23 Cromwell Street murders.

Closed in 1975, the jail is now owned by Andy Jones, who has worked hard to preserve the building and its contents.

Loseley Park House : Loseley Park, Guildford, Surrey†

Film: *The Legacy* (1978)

Following Henry VIII's dissolution of the monasteries, many of the abbeys became convenient quarries for local building projects. Much of the stone from Waverley Abbey in Surrey was used to create Sir William More's house at Loseley in the 1560s. His father had purchased the estate in 1508, continuing to live in the original medieval house until his death in 1549, but Sir William planned a grand new home fit for entertaining royalty. Built from the mellowed monastic stone, and other local materials, Loseley Park house was substantial, comfortably fitted out, adequately symbolizing the status of a queen's most trusted advisor.

Nearly 500 years later and Loseley Park House is still the ancestral home of the More family. A fine Elizabethan mansion, little changed structurally from the time it was built, the house contains many interesting artifacts collected through the different generations of the More family who have made it their home. From Sir William's time, his impressive wood-paneled library featuring

*www.littledeanjail.com. Written by Sally-Anne Ryan.
†www.loseleypark.co.uk.

an elaborately carved overmantel bearing the arms and initials of Elizabeth I in honor of her many visits to Loseley Park. Another frequent royal visitor was King James I, who gifted a painting of himself and Queen Anne to commemorate the visits. In 1932 Queen Mary was a visitor to Loseley.

Among the many rooms on display in the house, the most fascinating is the drawing room, with rich oak paneling, a gilded ceiling and frieze, and a magnificent carved chalk chimneypiece.

In 1978 Loseley doubled as Mountolive Manor for the horror movie *The Legacy*, in which a group of invited guests are brutally murdered one by one. What could be a more perfect setting for murder than an Elizabethan mansion?

Today the house and gardens are open to the public. The entire estate covers some 1400 acres, much of it given over to agricultural use.

Moor Park Mansion : Rickmansworth, Hertfordshire

Film: *The Vampire Lovers* (1970)

Doubling as the grand home of General Spielsdorf (Peter Cushing) in the Hammer horror *The Vampire Lovers*, Moor Park is a Grade 1–listed Palladian mansion set within several hundred acres of parkland in Hertfordshire. It is called Moor Park Mansion because it is in the old park of the Manor of More.

The original house was built in 1678 and '79 for James, duke of Monmouth, and inherited by his duchess after he was beheaded. Before her death (1732), Benjamin Hoskins Styles, who had made his fortune in the South Sea Company, purchased it. He then had it re-built (as it looks today) circa 1720 by Giacomo Leoni, using Portland stone and adding grand portico and Tuscan colonades. It was also given a painted staircase by Sir James Thornhill.

In 1752 it was bought by Admiral Lord Anson who commissioned Capability Brown to remake the formal gardens in sweeping "landscape style" with a small lake.

Further owners succeeded at regular intervals until 1928, when the enlarged estate was sold to the Grosvenor family headed by the earl of Grosvenor, son of the duke of Westminster.

During World War II the mansion was requisitioned, becoming the headquarters of the 1st Airborne Corps who planned Operation Market Garden.

In more recent years it has been used as a film location. Apart from its appearance in *The Vampire Lovers*, the mansion can also be seen in the action-adventure movie *The Hellfire Club* (1960), which also features Peter Cushing.

Today it contains the clubhouse for Moor Park Golf Club, and can be hired for celebrations and weddings.

New Lodge : Drift Road, Winkfield, Windsor, Berkshire

Films: *Asylum* (1972), *Trog* (1970)

New Lodge is located in the former Windsor forest, which has been recorded as a hunting ground since Anglo-Saxon times. The forest was at its largest in the Middle Ages with a circumference of 120 miles.

The name New Lodge first appears on a map in 1607, as one of the seven forest lodges built to entertain royal hunting parties. It is in fact one of the grandest hunting lodges, built in Italianate style.

During its first years, the lodge was owned by the monarchy and occupied by a number of different members of the royal family. In 1857 Jean Sylvain Van de Weyer redeveloped New Lodge into the prominent house which dominates the estate today. It was later enhanced by his son Victor into a 3,720-acre estate, including 16 farms, an inn, numerous cottages and extensive tracts of meadows and woods.

After Victor died in 1915 the house was sold to Barnardo's as an orphanage, and later during World War II was sublet as a house to accommodate refugees.

In 1956 the house became home to the British Transport Commission. In the early 1970s it was used as a film location. First it was seen as a scientific research center where Joan Crawford experiments on a newly discovered living apeman in *Trog*. Then it doubled as the Dunsmoor Mental Institution, in which Robert Powell would have to guess which inmate is the deranged Dr. Starr, a former employee who has a penchant for strangulation, in the horror thriller *Asylum*.

In 1972 the neo-gothic country house became office accommodations for the first time. It is presently owned by a commercial developer, Marchday Group plc.

Oakley Court : Windsor Road, Water Oakley, Windsor, Berkshire*

Films: *The Curse of Frankenstein* (1957), *Die Monster Die!* (1965), *Dracula* (1973), *The House in Nightmare Park* (1972), *The Mutations* (1974), *The Night Digger* (1971), *And Now the Screaming Starts!* (1972), *The Old Dark House* (1962), *The Rocky Horror Picture Show* (1975), *Vampyres* (1974), *Witchcraft* (1964)

Doubling as Carfax in the 1973 version of *Dracula* with Jack Palance playing the immortal count, and as the home to lesbian vampires in the cult

*www.oakleycourt.com.

classic *Vampyres* (1974), Oakley Court was by far the most frequently used of all the horror film locations.

It is situated along a stretch of the River Thames in Windsor, Berkshire, known as Water Oakley, and is indeed a delightful haven of Victorian Gothic splendor. It was originally built for Sir Richard Hall Say in 1859 in the style of a French chateau. Say, who married Ellen Evans of Boveney Court, Buckinghamshire, in 1857, was appointed high sheriff of Berkshire in 1864 and then justice of the peace in 1865.

In 1874 Oakley was sold to Lord Otto Fitzgerald, who then in turn would sell it to John Lewis Phipps. At the beginning of the twentieth century, the mansion was in the ownership of Sir William Avery. Ernest Olivier would purchase the property in 1919, together with 50 acres of Berkshire woodland, for the sum of £27,000. Olivier was a very eccentric character who frequently entertained foreign diplomats and, as a courteous gesture, flew the flag of the nation they represented on the original flagpole — which still stands today.

It is said that during World War II Oakley was used as the English headquarters for the French Resistance. President De Gaulle is reputed to have stayed in one of the mansion's bedrooms.

In 1955, Bray Film Studios moved to Down Place, just next door, and so for the next 24 years some 200 movies were made in and around the property. It became particularly busy film-wise in 1965, after the death of Mr. Olivier.

Numerous horror productions were shot at the mansion to give eerie Gothic effect. *And Now the Screaming Starts!* features the house as the ghostly House of Fengriffen, where an apparition frightens the soul out of newlywed Stephanie Beacham. In *The House in Nightmare Park*, Frankie Howerd is stalked along its dark corridors by his axe-wielding mad brother, Ray Milland; in *The Mutations*, Donald Pleasence is up to some nasty business in an attic room; and Boris Karloff hides a sinister secret in the basement in *Die Monster Die!* It has also though played the part of Chateau Frankenstein in *The Curse of Frankenstein*, and been home to some homicidals in *The Old Dark House* and some Satanists led by Lon Chaney, Jr., in *Witchcraft*. Peter Cushing (as Van Helsing) chased wicked Baron Meinster (David Peel) through its imposing grand entrance in *The Brides of Dracula*. *The Night Digger* saw a corrupt and evil young gardener, Nicholas Clay, plotting to murder two of the mansion's oldest residents.

Today it serves a more different purpose, as a busy hotel, and is open to reservations all year round. If you're lucky, you might on a moonlit night see the leering figure of Riff Raff (Richard O'Brien) peeking through one of the shadowy windows, as he did in *The Rocky Horror Picture Show*.

Witchfinder General: The climax of the film in which Hopkins takes Richard Marshall (Ian Ogilvy) and Sarah Lowes (Hilary Dwyer) to be tortured was filmed at Orford Castle, Orford, Suffolk. Courtesy of Orford Castle.

Orford Castle : Orford, Suffolk*

Film: *Witchfinder General* (1968)

Standing on the Suffolk coast, Orford Castle (built by King Henry II between 1165 and 1173) was positioned to ward off the threat of coastal invasions. When completed, the castle consisted of a curtain wall with a number of flanking towers, and a twin-towered gatehouse surrounding the Great Tower. A large ditch around the outside of the curtain wall provided further protection. The curtain wall, gatehouse and towers all decayed through neglect and nothing of them survives today.

Still standing, though, is the Great Tower of the original royal castle. This construction resembles no other in Britain or Ireland, with its basic plan of a circular tower, incorporating three great turrets (rising to some 90 feet high) spaced equidistantly around it.

Inside Orford Castle's thick stone walls, it is apparent that this was designed

*www.orford.org.uk.

to be a fortified family residence, with spiral stairs inside each of the towers leading to a maze of passageways.

At the first level is a wedge-shaped chapel. To the left of the doorway, a narrow gap at the edge of the floor shows this was used as a portcullis slot. In all, the Great Tower is five storeys high, with the first and second floors spanning two levels; the roof has battlemented parapets located between the three turrets that then rise above roof level.

For Michael Reeves' savage horror *Witchfinder General*, part of the basement was used as Matthew Hopkins's (Vincent Price's) torture chamber, where he interrogates Richard Marshall (Ian Ogilvy) and Sarah Lowes (Hilary Dwyer).

A strangely fascinating castle keep set among its former defense mounds and looking very much out of place today alongside a busy road, Orford is a magnificent attraction. It now stands open to the public, and for all those interested, the basement still holds some gruesome props from its horror film past.

Osterley Park House : Isleworth, Middlesex

Film: *A Study in Terror* (1965), *Jack the Ripper* (1988)

Osterley Park is a mansion set in a large parkland of the same name. It is now in the western suburbs of London, but when it was built it was in the country. It was one of a group of large houses close to London which served as country retreats for wealthy families, but were not true country houses on large agricultural estates.

The original building on this site was a manor house built for banker Sir Thomas Gresham in the sixteenth century. Queen Elizabeth visited twice, on one occasion suggesting that a hedge would be a good idea in a certain location. It was built overnight! The stable block from this period remains at Osterley Park.

Two hundred years later the manor house was falling into disrepair, when it came into the ownership of Sir Francis Child, a goldsmith turned banker, as a result of a mortgage default. In 1761 he employed Robert Adam, who was just emerging as one of the most fashionable architects in England, to remodel the house. The house of red brick with white stone details is approximately square, with turrets in four corners. Adam's design, which incorporates some of the earlier structure, is highly unusual, and differs greatly in style from the original construction. One side is left almost open and is spanned by an ionic portico which is approached by a broad flight of steps and leads to a central courtyard, which is piano nobile level.

Adam's neoclassical interiors are among his most notable sequences of rooms. The drawing room was described as "worthy of Eve before the fall." Adam also designed some of the furniture, including the opulent domed state bed, which is still in the house.

When Sir Francis Child died in 1763, the house was taken up by his brother and heir, Robert Child, who in turn left Osterley in his will to his eldest granddaughter, Lady Sarah Sophia Fane, who was born in 1785. She married George Child-Villiers, 5th earl of Jersey, and thus Osterley passed into the Jersey family. It was the 9th earl of Jersey who gave the house and much of the estate of the National Trust in 1949.

Osterley Park's grounds were used for the training of the first members of the Local Defense Volunteers (who later became the British Home Guard) in 1940.

In 1965 director James Hill used Osterley Park to double as the home of the duke of Shires in his Sherlock Holmes–Jack the Ripper shocker, *A Study In Terror*. Its courtyard doubled beautifully as the Royal Mews in *Jack the Ripper*, a superb David Wickes production with Michael Caine.

It is presently open to the public, and contains most of the original furniture in excellent condition.

Parham House : Storrington, Nr. Pulborough, West Sussex*

Film: *Haunted* (1995)

Parham is a beautiful Elizabethan house set in an ancient deer park. During the Middle Ages the manor of Parham was owned by Westminster Abbey. In 1540 Parham was given to Robert Palmer, a London mercer, by Henry VIII. His son, Sir Thomas Palmer, began to build a new house at Parham in 1577, incorporating parts of the old manor house. The present house remains essentially as it was built then.

In 1601 Parham was sold to Thomas Bysshop and the property remained in the hands of the same family until the twentieth century, when it was sold to the Hon. Clive Pearson. He would purchase many of the Bysshop family's paintings and added his own collection of portraits, as well as English furniture. After his death in 1965 the property was vested in the Parham Park Trust but the house is still the home of his eldest daughter, P.A. Tritton.

A long drive approaches Parham through a wooded deer park, with the house standing on broad lawns, with parkland on all sides. The picturesque house is built of gray stone with varied gables and chimneys.

The entrance hall is hung with eighteenth century portraits and equestrian paintings. A flight of steps leads you on to the upper hall, and from here to the Great Hall. This room, rising through two storeys, is one of the most magnificent Elizabethan rooms in Britain, with beautiful old oak English furniture, and walls hung with a splendid collection of sixteenth century portraits,

*www.parhaminsussex.co.uk

Haunted: Doubling as the haunted manor house, "Edbrook Hall," is Parham House, Storrington, Nr. Pulborough, West Sussex. Courtesy of Simon Flynn.

including Elizabeth I, and a remarkable allegorical equestrian portrait of Henry, prince of Wales.

It's certainly the place for a professor seeking out ghostly phenomenon. Aidan Quinn goes there to seek out some spiritual goings-on in the film *Haunted*. But does he actually find anything...?

Why don't you go there yourself? It's open to the public all year round.

St. Michael's Mount : Marazion, Cornwall*

Film: *Dracula* (1979)

According to legend, St. Michael's Mount was built by a giant called Cormoran, whose wife brought the greenstone in her apron. One version of the legend says that the giant would wade ashore and snatch up livestock from local farms and then take them back with him, but finally slipped and fell to his death and is buried under the pile of greenstone you can still find there today.

As you walk up to the castle, you will come across a heart-shaped stone on the pathway; legend says that if you stand on this stone you can still hear the giant's heartbeat. Another legend suggests that the giant was actually killed by a young boy called Jack and that this is the basis of the "Jack the Giant Killer"

*www.stmichaelsmount.co.uk. Written by Brian Holland.

fairy story. Yet another legend says that it is the giant's wife who is buried under the greenstone.

St. Michael's Mount was a trading post for tin and copper from as early as 350 BC but very little of this early history is known. It is believed that it was an important trading post and generally believed to be the island of Ictis mentioned by the Greeks, who traded there for Cornish tin.

In 490 AD it was visited by St. Keyne during his travels and the story goes that in 495 AD the archangel St. Michael appeared to a group of fishermen at the mount, standing high on a rocky ledge on the western side of the mount.

Edward the Confessor founded a chapel on the mount in 1044 and gave this to the Benedictine monks who built a priory on the summit and also constructed the harbor and the causeway which leads to the mainland at low tide.

During the twelfth century, while King Richard I was on a crusade in the Holy Land, the mount was seized and held as a fortress by a group of his brother John's supporters. Henry VIII took possession when he dissolved the monasteries and it was subsequently used as a fortress during the Civil War as a Royalist stronghold. One of the commanders of the Parliamentarian forces that captured the mount, Colonel John St. Aubyn, bought it from the state in 1659 and one of his descendants still lives there today.

St. Michael's Mount was given to the National Trust in 1954 and the castle and its grounds were opened to the public.

It has also had its time as a film location, featuring as Castle Dracula in the opening credits of John Badham's lavish screen version of the Bram Stoker novel.

Today it is possible to take a tour through the castle, including the fourteenth century church. The causeway to the mount is exposed at low tide, allowing you to walk across by foot. Otherwise there are small boats that run to and from the mainland, but with this and the steep climb up to the mount it is advisable to wear sturdy footwear.

St. Paul's Cathedral : Ludgate Hill, London*

Film: *Hands of the Ripper* (1971)

Building work on St. Paul's Cathedral began in June 1675. It replaced Old St. Paul's, which was gutted in the Great Fire of London in 1666, and is generally reckoned to be London's fourth St. Paul's Cathedral, the first being a Saxon Cathedral built in 604 AD.

The present St. Paul's with its large central dome, and towers at the west end, was designed by Sir Christopher Wren. The cathedral was completed on Wren's seventy-sixth birthday (October 20, 1708).

*www.stpauls.co.uk.

Hands of the Ripper: Featuring at the climax of the film is St. Paul's Cathedral, Ludgate Hill, London. (Photograph by the author.)

The cathedral is built of Portland stone in a late renaissance style. Its impressive dome was inspired by St. Peter's Basilica in Rome. It rises 365 feet to the cross at the summit, making it a famous London landmark.

The main space inside the cathedral is centered under the dome. This rises 108.4 meters from the cathedral floor and holds three circular galleries — the internal Whispering Gallery, the external Stone Gallery, and the external Golden Gallery.

The Whispering Gallery runs around the interior of the dome and is 259 steps up from ground level. A whisper against its wall at any point is audible to a listener with their ear held to the point diametrically opposite.

In the northwest tower there are 13 bells, while the southwest tower contains four bells, including Great Paul, which was cast in 1881, and Great Tom (the hour bell), which has been recast twice after being removed from the old palace of Westminster.

The cathedral's organ was first commissioned in 1694 and the current instrument is the third biggest in Britain with 7,189 pipes and 138 stops.

St. Paul's has survived until the present day despite being targeted during the Blitz (it was struck by bombs on October 10, 1940 and April 17, 1941, but survived).

The cathedral is the home of plaques, carvings, statues, memorials, and tombs of famous British figures, including the duke of Wellington, Admiral Nelson, Sir Winston Churchill and Florence Nightingale.

Even though the Royal Family prefers to use Westminster Abbey for important marriages, christenings, and funerals, St. Paul's was used for the marriage of Charles, Prince of Wales, to Lady Diana Spencer in 1981.

St. Paul's has also on occasion been a film location, most notably in David Lean's *Great Expectations* (1946) and *Lawrence of Arabia* (1962). It is also seen at the end of the film *The Madness of King George* (1994).

For horror movie fans it is best remembered for its appearance at the climax of one of Hammer's better 1970s offerings, *Hands of the Ripper*, in which Dr. Pritchard (Eric Porter) saves Laura (Jane Merrow) from a murderous Anna (Angharad Rees) in the Whispering Gallery. The interior of the cathedral had to be recreated on sound stages at Pinewood Studios, because Hammer Films was not granted permission to shoot inside. However, the exterior is the real thing.

The cathedral is open daily to the public, though there is a charge for non-worshipping visitors.

Somerset House : Strand, London*

Films: *Jack the Ripper* (1988), *Jekyll & Hyde* (1989), *Sleepy Hollow* (1999)

Somerset House has been at the heart of English history since the sixteenth century.

The first Somerset House was built by Edward Seymour ("Protector Somerset") in 1547, and was celebrated as the first Renaissance building on any scale in England.

Following Somerset's execution, it became a Royal palace, primarily occupied by queens and their courts, which gave Somerset House a reputation for royal extravagance and debauchery.

By contrast, Oliver Cromwell lay in state at Somerset House. However, during the eighteenth century the old palace gradually fell into disrepair, and in 1775 Sir William Chambers was commissioned by George III to rebuild Somerset House on the site of the early Tudor palace. Chambers decided to build an elaborate columned vestibule, leading to a more spacious courtyard beyond.

The strand block (now home to the Courtauld Institute of Art and its gallery) was built to house the learned societies: the Royal Academy, the Royal Society and the Society of Antiquaries.

The vestibule is decorated with splendid neo-classical plasterwork befitting those noble organizations. Busts of Michelangelo and Sir Isaac Newton stand over the doorway of the Royal Academy and Royal Society.

The bronze statue in the courtyard was erected in 1789 and represents George III.

Somerset House itself was built to house some of the most important government departments, including the Inland Revenue. Most of the building is open to the public as a place of enjoyment, refreshment, arts and culture. Between the months of November and January the courtyard becomes home to a beautiful skating rink.

For many years now Somerset House has been a regular film and televi-

*www.somerset-house.org.uk.

sion location. It was featured in two James Bond movies, *GoldenEye* (1995) and *Tomorrow Never Dies* (1997). It has also turned up in classic films like *The Day of the Jackal* (1973) and Billy Wilder's *The Private Life of Sherlock Holmes* (1970).

As regards horror productions, it has featured in three. First it was the exterior of Guy's Hospital in the excellent David Wickes film *Jack the Ripper* (1988). Then, in 1989, the courtyard of Somerset House doubled as a Victorian London Street in *Jekyll & Hyde* starring Michael Caine (also directed by David Wickes). In 1999, the courtyard doubled as a New York street in Tim Burton's gothic *Sleepy Hollow* with Johnny Depp.

Stanmore Hall : Wood Lane, Stanmore, Middlesex

Films: *Frankenstein Must Be Destroyed* (1969), *Nothing But the Night* (1972)

Built in 1843 by Matthew John Rhodes, Stanmore is a splendid Gothic pile, replete with battlements and turrets. The architect was John Macduff Derick. Some of the interiors are the workmanship of famous British architect William Morris.

One of the finest features of the original hall was a beautiful Gothic library rather sparsely furnished with hundreds of books.

In 1917 Stanmore turned from being a private house. It is said to have been used as an assize court, and then as flats in the 1930s. During the second world war it was the officers' mess for the staff of the Allied Expeditionary Air Force, and known irreverently by them as Gremlin Castle.

From 1947 to 1971 it was used as a nurses' home for the Royal National Orthopaedic Hospital. After this time its fate hung in the balance and many people feared that it would be demolished and the site redeveloped, especially after a fire in 1979. Local pressure and a changing attitude towards conservation prevailed and the house was sympathetically restored and converted into offices.

It was during Stanmore's difficult period that many television productions were shot there, including *Randall & Hopkirk (Deceased)*, *The Professionals*, and several episodes of the cult British television series *The Avengers*, including "From Venus with Love" and "The Winged Avenger."

Horror film productions also made use of its Gothic splendor. It doubled as the home of Baron Frankenstein (Peter Cushing) in Hammer's *Frankenstein Must Be Destroyed*, and also featured as Inver House, an orphanage full of demonic children, in *Nothing but the Night*.

Recently, the Hall was sold again, and thus became what it is today — luxurious apartments.

Thorpe House : Coldharbour Lane, Thorpe, Surrey

Films: *Craze* (1974), *The Creeping Flesh* (1972)

Thorpe House was built between 1717 and 1745 by Richard Bartholomew, with additions in 1750 by its new owner, Isaac Townsend, a retired admiral of the Navy and member of Parliament.

At this time it was a fine brick structure with a "modern" neo-classical Georgian facade. The typical features are the small window balconies, the decorative brickwork, and the arched portico over the front door.

In 1789 Thorpe House was bought by a Major Scott. Members of the Scott family resided there up until the 1940s.

Between 1942 and 1945 the War Office took possession of Thorpe House for the purposes of training specialist military personnel (up to 100 were housed there). They were instructed on receiving and transmitting services, and reading and typing Morse code.

After the war Thorpe House remained empty for five years in a poor state of repair. In 1950 it was sold by a son-in-law of the Scott family to a Mr. Williams, who made his fortune as a wholesale greengrocer. He allowed film companies to shoot on the premises, and it was during this time that two horror films were partially shot there (both directed by Freddie Francis). The first was the Victorian chiller *The Creeping Flesh*, in which as Peter Cushing's home it would hide the remains of a sinister Neanderthal man, holding a deadly secret. Jack Palance sacrificed his own aunt to a voodoo god in the house's beautiful gardens in *Craze*.

In 1976 the American School in England became the tenant, and Thorpe House continues to be home to them to this day.

The Vyne : Sherborne St. John, Basingstoke*

Film: *The Black Torment* (1964)

The Vyne was built in the sixteenth century for Lord Sandys, Henry VIII's lord chamberlain. It then became home to the Chute family for more than 300 years. Through the artistic and aesthetic interests of its various owners, it has been at the cutting edge of the development of country house architecture, interior design and taste.

Like many medieval foundations, The Vyne stands on low-lying ground and near water. This was transformed into a spectacular lake setting for the north front of the building in the eighteenth century. The irregular pattern of brickwork, ranging in color from pale to deep red, reveals how much the exterior has been altered over the centuries.

*Written by Brian Holland.

In the mid–seventeenth century it acquired the classical portico on the north front. In the late eighteenth century a dramatic Palladian staircase hall was designed by the owner, John Chute.

Other interesting features at The Vyne include the double galleries, one set above the other. The upper Oak Gallery is one of the very few long galleries surviving from the first half of the sixteenth century and the most richly decorated. Each of the linen-fold oak panels is embellished with carved emblems of the senior figures of the court of Henry VIII and his first wife Catherine of Aragon.

In the early nineteenth century, The Vyne entered a period of neglect, which actually helped to preserve its ancient interiors. When a more active owner, William Wiggett Chute, took up residence in 1842, he modernized the services, but it is typical of the family that he fitted out his new library upstairs with a seventeenth century chimney-piece and woodwork.

Sir Charles Chute, first baronet, gave the house together with its historic contents and estate to the National Trust in 1956, so that they could be preserved for the nation. During this time it has been used as a film location, and doubles as Fordyke Hall, the home of Sir Richard Fordyke (John Turner), a man verging on insanity, in the chiller *The Black Torment*.

The Vyne is presently open to the public.

Westminster Abbey : Westminster, London*

Film: *The Quatermass Xperiment* (1955)

Westminster Abbey is probably better known to most people for its royal occasions rather than for its film connections. Steeped in history, it holds the tombs of numerous kings and queens and the shrine of Edward the Confessor, dating back to the thirteenth century. It has also been the setting for every coronation since 1066. Today it remains a church to worship and the place where we still celebrate great events in history.

In the 1040s, King Edward, later St. Edward the Confessor, last of the Anglo-Saxon kings, chose to re-endow and enlarge a small Benedictine monastery close to his royal palace by the banks of the River Thames. This church became known as the "west Minster" as opposed to St. Paul's Cathedral which was known as the "east Minster" in the city of London. When the church was finally consecrated on December 28, 1065, the king was too ill to attend and died a few days later. His remains are entombed in front of the High Altar. The only evidence of this monastery now can be found in the round arches and supporting columns of the Undercroft in the Cloisters of the Westminster Abbey.

*www.westminsterabbey.org. Written by Sally-Anne Ryan.

Edwards Abbey survived until the middle of the thirteenth century when King Henry III decided to re-build it in the new gothic style of architecture. This was a great time for cathedrals in England, Canterbury, Winchester, and Salisbury were also constructed during this time. Under the decree of the King of England, Westminster Abbey was designed to be a great monastery and place of worship and also a place for coronation and the burial of monarchs.

Over three thousand people are buried within Westminster Abbey and it contains around 600 monuments and wall tablets. People buried there include Henry III, Edward I, Richard II, Henry V, Elizabeth I, Charles Dickens, Henry Irving, and Sir Laurence Olivier.

Westminster Abbey has on occasion been a film location, and that once included a horror production. Hammer's *The Quatermass Xperiment* climaxed at the Abbey, with the alien creature being cornered and incinerated within its walls.

A historic and beautiful building, Westminster Abbey will no doubt remain popular with filmmakers wishing to recreate scenes in times gone by. In 2005 the makers of *The Da Vinci Code* were denied access as it was felt the story was theologically unsound. The filming was moved to Lincoln Cathedral where the Chapter House was transformed to resemble the Abbey.

Whitby : North Yorkshire

Film: *Count Dracula* (1977)

Whitby is an ancient seaport and fishing town on the northeast coast of England. It has been a haven for holiday-makers since Victorian times and has played a significant role in English history. Its harbor, once the sixth largest port in Britain, lies where the River Esk reaches the North Sea.

Whitby's skyline is dominated by St. Hilda's Abbey, which was founded in 657 AD by the Saxon King of Northumbria, Oswy (Oswiu) as Streanshalh (Streonshalh). He appointed Lady Hilda, niece of Edwin, the first Christian King of Northumbria, as Abbess. The double monastery of Benedictine monks and nuns was also home to the great Saxon poet Caedmon. In 664, the abbey, built on the east cliff overlooking the Esk and town of Whitby, was the site of the Synod of Whitby, at which the Northumbrian Celtic church was reconciled to Rome. However, in 867, the abbey fell to Viking attack, and was abandoned until 1078, when it was re-founded by Regenfrith (Reinferd), a soldier monk, under the orders of his protector, the Norman William de Percy.

This second monastery lasted until it was destroyed by Henry VIII in 1540. The abbey fell into ruins, and was subsequently mined for stone, but remains a prominent landmark for sailors to this day.

*www.whitby.co.uk.

There is no doubt at all that Whitby, the ruined Abbey and the nearby St. Mary's graveyard had a profound effect on Bram Stoker while he was writing his novel *Dracula*, for he was staying at the Royal Hotel on the western side of the town at the time. There are many references in his book which are clearly taken from the view that Stoker had from the hotel, looking towards East Cliff; this view obviously inspired his fertile imagination. Three-quarters of his story is set around Whitby and it is still possible to retrace those steps of the undead, taking the Dracula Trail Tour. There is even a Bram Stoker memorial seat perched high up on West Cliff.

Even though the town plays a prominent role in Stoker's story, and its name was first immortalized on the silver screen in Universal's *Dracula* starring Bela Lugosi in 1931, the town itself has only ever appeared in one filmed version of the gothic novel, and that was the BBC Films adaptation *Count Dracula* starring Louis Jourdan (1977).

Count Dracula: Doubling as Whitby for the first time in any Dracula film production is Whitby, North Yorkshire. (Photograph by the author.)

Wilton's Music Hall : Graces Alley, Ensign Street, Whitechapel, London*

Film: *Interview with the Vampire* (1994)

As an actor, and writer of this book, I found Wilton's by far the most interesting place I visited. It is full of atmosphere and, even though it has decayed slightly over the years, it still stands as a very beautiful piece of theatrical heritage.

It is the world's oldest surviving grand music hall; in the 1850s and '60s the classical overtures, opera and operetta, choral, contemporary and folk songs were enormously popular there, long before "old-time music hall" evolved.

*www.wiltons.org.uk.

John Wilton built the theatre behind his public house, The Prince of Denmark, in 1858, and it would be described as the "handsomest room in town."

A sun-burner chandelier with 300 gas jets and 27,000 cut crystals dominated a mirrored hall where George Leybourne (Champagne Charlie) sang. Rumor has it that the first ever can-can was performed (and was promptly banned) at Wilton's.

Today, the auditorium remains incredibly intact. The original cast iron "barley sugar" pillars support a papier-mâché balcony under paper roses set in a vaulted roof.

In Wilton's day, 1,500 people used to cram into the music hall to hear the top acts; artistes from the Royal Opera House were lured over in full costume to perform late night favorite arias. Today the hall has a license to seat 300 people.

In 1880 John Wilton died at age 60. Wilton's continued as a music hall until 1884, when it was taken over by the East End Mission of the Methodist Church, who would remain there until 1956. During World War II, they gave shelter to a badly blitzed community. From the late fifties until the early sixties, Wilton's was used as a rag warehouse.

In 1964 Sir John Betjeman campaigned to make the music hall a listed building to prevent its demolition; many people helped in saving it, including Laurence Olivier, Peter Sellers and Liza Minnelli. Wilton's was therefore given a Grade II listing.

In the 1990s, the music hall would become a frequent film location, and can be seen in such movies as *The Krays* (1990), and Lord Attenborough's *Chaplin* (1992). It has also played its part in horror film history, as a scene for the gothic *Interview with the Vampire* with Tom Cruise and Brad Pitt was partly filmed there.

2004 saw the newly formed Wilton's Music Hall Trust begin a restoration drive. The public can now experience and appreciate the heritage of Wilton's through a variety of media, such as performance, heritage education, guided tours and events.

Over 2,000 children of all ages have explored the theatre through heritage, music, drama, history, art and design workshops. Since 2004, 3,500 people have come through the theatre's doors for guided tours.

To end on an eerie note: During Wilton's music hall heyday in the late nineteenth century, it's possible that Jack the Ripper may have once sat in the audience at this Whitechapel theatre.

Wyfold Court : Rotherfield Peppard, Henley-on-Thames, Oxfordshire

Film: *Funny Man* (1994)

This Grade II-listed mansion near Henley-on-Thames presents a magnificent façade, being built of red brick with ornate blue brick diapering and stone

Funny Man: Featuring as the Chance Manor, the ancestral home of Callum Chance (Christopher Lee), is Wyfold Court, Rotherfield Peppard, Henley-on-Thames, Oxfordshire. Courtesy of Simon Flynn.

detailing. The front is recessed with a porte-cochere and corner turreted tower in one wing and a larger steep roofed tower in the other, while tracery windows abound. Gargoyles and pinnacles help to make up a dramatic silhouette against the skyline to show off its flamboyant French Gothic style, with a feel of the Scottish Baronial, to perfection. To the rear, bay windows are the main feature while carved heraldic beasts can be seen on the gables, as ornamentation.

Is it any wonder then that it was chosen to double as the ancestral home of Callum Chance (Christopher Lee), a manor house hiding a demonic and murderous jester, in the horror comedy *Funny Man*.

Wyfold was built between 1872 and 1878 for Edward Hermon, a wealthy Lancastrian cotton master, MP for Preston and a lavish patron of contemporary artists.

Much later, after a period as a hospital, this superb Victorian mansion was completely restored to its original splendiferous appearance both inside and out. This included painstaking restoration on the stone vaulted corridors, marbled pillars and pavement, Gothic revivalist ceilings and fireplaces.

Described by architectural historian Peter Howell as "one of the most coherent, carefully detailed and inventive houses built in Victorian times," Wyfold now has eleven new luxurious properties within its walls.

Wykehurst Place : Wykehurst Park, Bolney, West Sussex

Films: *Demons of the Mind* (1972), *The Legend of Hell House* (1973), *Son of Dracula* (1974)

Probably the most haunting of all the film locations is Wykehurst. Here, Simon Flynn reveals its history and tells us about his visits to this granddaddy of manor houses:

When Derek sent me the list of locations to hunt out, one was of real interest, Hell House (Wykehurst Place), not just because of the notoriety of the film *The Legend of Hell House*, but mainly because of its closeness to my own home, literally down the road — at most, five miles away. I set out one Sunday lunchtime when it was cold but very sunny. Driving my car up a windy rural country lane, I came to an iron gate. Here was a pathway with hedges on either side. I walked down it, and could see there was a large house behind two stone pillars (each with a griffin on top, looking down at me, watching my every move). Nothing could have prepared me for what I saw next. Yes, there was no mistaking this one, this must be Hell House. I looked on in awe; in fact, it almost took my breath away, and made me swear out loud at first seeing it (a sort of "bloody hell" or much worse).

Despite it being a sunny afternoon, I felt uneasy and I honestly had the hairs on my arms standing on end.

A couple of weeks later I returned, only this time it was at night. Now you have to remember that there is no house visible nearby, it is surrounded by green trees and hedges and there are no street lights. So it's pitch black, almost in a forest. I parked my car, walked up the path, caught sight of the turrets, and said to myself, "I can't go any further." Plucking up courage, though, I crossed the threshold of the griffins, and looked up at the house. After swearing, I quickly hurried back to the car.

This sums it up: It looks so overblown it its sinister gothic style as if it was a castle in mid–Bavaria, not mid–Sussex. It could even be the type of haunted house you would expect to see in a Disneyland theme park, as it just has that unrealness about it. The thing which is most spooky about it is that despite its hugeness, it remains hidden from the front pathway, even as you walk further down; then suddenly, it's right there in front of you, larger than life. It just hits you, when you don't expect it, and surpasses any shot of it in *The Legend of Hell House*.

Wykehurst Place was built in 1872 by Edward Middleton Barry (1830–1880), third son of Sir Charles Barry. Edward completed his father's work on

A sketch of a horror film location, Wykehurst Place, Wykehurst Park, Bolney, West Sussex. Courtesy of Wykehurst Place.

the Houses of Parliament, and he built the theatre of the Royal Opera House in Covent Garden, as well as the Great Ormond Street Hospital for sick children (which has now been demolished). The latter was built in 1872, the same year he built Hell House (Wykehurst Place), which some consider his finest achievement.

The house was built entirely of stone quarried in the immediate locality, and is a weird hodgepodge of architectural influences. The inspiration stemmed mainly from the huge chateaux of the Loire valley, but there is certainly more than a touch of Bavarian influence. (*Demons of the Mind*, another film shot there, was supposed to be set in the rural forests of Bavaria.)

Even over 100 years ago it cost well over £300,000 to build, and the work took 500 men nearly five years. When completed, with its towers, pinnacles, turrets and windows, it had a magnificent 105 rooms.

The first person to live there was Henry Huth, a German banker. He died four years after the house was completed.

"The Big House" (as Wykehurst was known) was the scene of many village festivities. There were hunt balls every year, and feasts on special village occasions. The coronation of King George V was celebrated in style at Wykehurst.

But the grandeur did not last. The library at Wykehurst once housed the finest private collection of books in Europe, but in 1910 they all had to be sold to pay for the house's upkeep.

Doubling as the menacing "Hell House," the Mount Everest of haunted houses, is Wykehurst Place, Bolney, West Sussex. Courtesy of Simon Flynn.

Between the wars it became a hotel and it is said that Edward VII and Mrs. Simpson stayed there on more than one occasion. During the second world war the house became a headquarters for the Allied invasion of Normandy, and was visited on one occasion by Eisenhower.

At the end of the war, the house became disused, and for many years stood derelict. And that's where Mr. Doyle comes in. An antiques dealer looking for a place in the country, he came across the run-down mansion and made his first attempt to buy it in 1957. The deal fell through, but every year he improved his offer and finally succeeded in buying the house and six acres of land around it in 1970. Mr. Doyle was to discover that the many years had brought severe dereliction to the house. He said, "I bought it as a ruin — outside walls. There were holes in the roof you could drive a car through, as thieves had stolen lead from it by the lorry load. Vandals had slashed to ribbons the French tapestries that had hung in the drawing room. The ground floor was piled with hay, and there was obvious evidence that the house had seen use as a cow-byre."

Mr. Doyle, with a team of 20 craftsmen, invented his own methods of repairing all the damage, and restoring the house and grounds to their former glory.

In *The Legend of Hell House*, the house is the monster. It's a powerful film and has no big star in the cast (the star was the house). It is the Mount Everest of British haunted house films, and they could not have chosen a better location. You really do believe that it's an evil house. You certainly wouldn't want to turn your back on it if you were gardening on the grounds.

I have heard from a local resident that it is supposedly haunted, and that a ghostly grey-green lady appears. If you catch sight of her, you are doomed to a horrible death.

Recently, I saw the house again in the daytime, and it seems even more grand than I initially thought. I've come to terms with its scariness, and can now appreciate it as the magnificent-looking house it is, stunningly beautiful and unique, with many deer grazing on its grounds.

As of this writing, Wykehurst remains a private residence.

What Was Filmed Where?

Avon
The Hole (Bath)

Berkshire
And Now the Screaming Starts! (Windsor)
Asylum (Windsor)
Blind Terror (Binfield)
The Brides of Dracula (Windsor)
The Curse of Frankenstein (Windsor)
Die Monster Die (Windsor)
Dracula (1958) (Bray)
Dracula (1973) (Windsor)
Frankenstein: The True Story (Bray)
The House in Nightmare Park (Windsor)
The Mummy (Bray)
The Mutations (Windsor)
The Night Digger (Windsor)
The Old Dark House (Windsor)
The Quatermass Xperiment (Bray)
The Rocky Horror Picture Show (Windsor)
Trog (Windsor)
Vampyres (Windsor)
Witchcraft (Windsor)

Buckinghamshire
The Black Cat (Hambleden)
Carry On Screaming (Wexham)
Dead of Night (Weston Turville)
Dracula Has Risen from the Grave (Wexham)
The Ghoul 1974 (Iver Heath)
Island of Terror (Gerrards Cross)
Legend of the Werewolf (Wexham)
The Masks of Death (Gerrards Cross)
Night of the Big Heat (Milton Keynes)
Persecution (Denham Village)
The Plague of the Zombies (Wexham)
Sleepy Hollow (Hambleden)
To the Devil a Daughter (West Wycombe)
Twins of Evil (Wexham)
The Watcher in the Woods (Gerrards Cross)

Cambridge
The Nightcomers (Sawston)

Cornwall
Crucible of Terror (St. Agnes)
Doomwatch (Polperro)
Dracula (1979) (Tintagel)
Straw Dogs (Trevowhan)
The Witches (Newquay)

Cumbria
Killer's Moon (Keswick)

Derbyshire
The Living Dead at the Manchester Morgue (Hathersage)

Essex
Quatermass 2 (Stanford-le-Hope)

Gloucestershire
House of Whipcord (Royal Forest of Dean)

Hampshire
The Black Torment (Basingstoke)
House of the Long Shadows (East Tisted)

Hertfordshire
The Abominable Dr. Phibes (Bushey)
The Anniversary (Borehamwood)
Castle Sinister (Bushey)
A Clockwork Orange (Shenley)
The Devil Rides Out (Elstree)
Fear in the Night (Aldenham)
Gothic (Hemel Hempstead)
Horror Hospital (Knebworth)
The Lair of the White Worm (Hemel Hempstead)
Lust for a Vampire (Kings Langley)
The Monster Club (Knebworth)
Night of the Demon (Welwyn)
The Satanic Rites of Dracula (Well End)
The Shining (Borehamwood)
The Vampire Lovers (Rickmansworth)
Village of the Damned (Letchmore Heath)

Kent
Inseminoid (Chislehurst)

Lincolnshire
The Haunting (1999) (Grantham)

London
The Awakening (Euston)
Blood Beast Terror (Harrow Weald)
Children of the Damned (St. Dunstans Hill)
Creep (Charing Cross)
Cry of the Banshee (Harrow Weald)
The Curse of the Crimson Altar (Harrow Weald)
Death Line (Russell Square)
Dr. Terror's House of Horrors (King's Cross)
Dracula A.D. 1972 (Chelsea)
Dream Demon (Hampstead)
Edge of Sanity (Clapham)
The Elephant Man (Tower Hill)
Endless Night (Harrow Weald)
Frankenstein and the Monster from Hell (Highgate)
Frenzy (Covent Garden)
From Beyond the Grave (Highgate)
The Ghoul (1933) (Shepherd's Bush)
Hands of the Ripper (St. Paul's)
Haunted House of Horror (Harrow Weald)
Hellraiser (Dollis Hill)
The Hunger (Bloomsbury)
I Don't Want to Be Born (Chelsea)
Interview with the Vampire (Whitechapel)
Jack the Ripper (Westminster)
Jekyll & Hyde (Strand)
Long Time Dead (Bermondsey)
The Mummy Returns (Euston)
The Nanny (Regent's Park)
Peeping Tom (Tottenham Court Road)
The Phantom of the Opera (Wimbledon)
Repulsion (Kensington)
Secret Ceremony (Kensington)
Shaun of the Dead (New Cross)
The Sorcerers (Marylebone)

Taste the Blood of Dracula (Highgate)
10 Rillington Place (Notting Hill)
Theatre of Blood (Kensal Green)
Theatre of Death (Hammersmith)
Vault of Horror (Westminster)

Middlesex

The Beast Must Die (Shepperton)
Frankenstein Must Be Destroyed (Stanmore)
Nothing but the Night (Stanmore)
Prey (Shepperton)
A Study in Terror (Isleworth)
Tales from the Crypt (Shepperton)

Norfolk

The Tomb of Ligeia (Swaffham)

Oxfordshire

Blood on Satan's Claw (Bix)
Funny Man (Rotherfield Peppard)

Scotland

The Descent (Pitlochry)
The Wicker Man (Dumfries & Galloway)

Suffolk

Witchfinder General (Orford)

Surrey

The Asylum (Coulsdon)
The Comeback (Cobham)
Craze (Thorpe)
The Creeping Flesh (Thorpe)
Frankenstein Created Woman (Frensham)
The Hound of the Baskervilles (Frensham)

House of Mortal Sin (Esher)
The House That Dripped Blood (Weybridge)
The Legacy (Guildford)
Madhouse (Pyrford)
Mother Riley Meets the Vampire (Walton-on-Thames)
The Mystery of the Mary Celeste (Walton-on-Thames)
The Omen (Pyrford)
Satan's Slave (Pirbright)
Virgin Witch (Pirbright)

Sussex

The Beast in the Cellar (Uckfield)
Demons of the Mind (Bolney)
The Flesh and Blood Show (Brighton)
Frightmare (Fernhurst)
Haunted (Storrington)
The Innocents (Sheffield Park)
The Legend of Hell House (Bolney)
Son of Dracula (Bolney)

Wales

An American Werewolf in London (Crickadarn)
Half Light (Porth Dinllaen)

Warwickshire

The Haunting (1963) (Stratford-on-Avon)

Wiltshire

28 Days Later (Salisbury)

Yorkshire

Count Dracula (Whitby)
Frankenstein (Harrogate)
Omen III—The Final Conflict (Ripon)

Hammer House of Horror

It was never my intention to include a television series within the pages of this book, but one does deserve a special mention, as it brought many happy hours of entertainment to me as an eight-year-old child, when it was first transmitted on British TV in 1980. The series in question had thirteen (of course) one-hour spine-tingling innovative bedtime horror stories. It was *Hammer House of Horror*, a series which is still as entertaining today as it was twenty-six years ago. It was produced by ITC Entertainment & Hammer Films with producer Roy Skeggs in charge.

The thirteen episodes were "Witching Time" (with Patricia Quinn and Jon Finch, directed by Don Leaver), "Thirteenth Reunion" (with Norman Bird, directed by Leaver), "Rude Awakening" (with Denholm Elliott, directed by Peter Sasdy), "Charlie Boy" (with Leigh Lawson and Marius Goring, directed by Robert Young), "Children of the Full Moon" (with Diana Dors and Robert Urquhart, directed by Tom Clegg), "The Carpathian Eagle" (with Pierce Brosnan, directed by Francis Megahy), "Guardian of the Abyss" (with John Carson and Barbara Ewing, directed by Don Sharp), "Growing Pains" (with Barbara Kellerman and Norman Beaton, directed by Megahy), "The House That Bled to Death" (with Nicholas Ball and Rachel Davies, directed by Clegg), "The Silent Scream" (with Peter Cushing and Brian Cox, directed by Alan Gibson), "The Two Faces of Evil" (with Gary Raymond, directed by Alan Gibson), "The Mark of Satan" (with Peter McEnery, directed by Leaver) and "Visitor from the Grave" (with Simon MacCorkindale, directed by Sasdy).

As regards locations, there is one which was used throughout the series, and that is the fourteenth century Hampden House in Great Hampden, Nr. Great Missenden, Buckinghamshire. This large, stately home can be seen during the creepy opening credits sequence, as well as in the episodes "Thirteenth Reunion," doubling as the Health Club; "Charlie Boy," where it doubled as the home of Graham's (Leigh Lawson) uncle, and "Children of the Full Moon," doubling as the sinister home of Mrs. Ardoy (Diana Dors).

Top: *Hammer House of Horror*: Hampden House, Great Hampden, Nr. Great Missenden, Buckinghamshire, can be seen during the opening credits of each episode, and also features in the episode "Charlie Boy." Courtesy of Simon Flynn. Bottom: *Hammer House of Horror*: Hampden House Church, Great Hampden, Nr. Great Missenden, Buckinghamshire, can be seen in the episode "Witching Time." Courtesy of Simon Flynn.

Top: *Hammer House of Horror*: The ordinary-looking house which hides a sinister secret in the episode "The House That Bled to Death" can be found on Chairborough Road, High Wycombe, Buckinghamshire. Courtesy of Simon Flynn. Bottom: *Hammer House of Horror*: The pet shop owned by Peter Cushing in the episode "The Silent Scream" can be found at 68 Broad Street, Chesham, Buckinghamshire. Courtesy of Simon Flynn.

Hampden House Church, which stands in the same grounds as Hampden House, can be seen briefly in the episode "Witching Time."

In one of the more popular episodes, "The House That Bled to Death," the ordinary-looking house where blood oozes from a burst pipe over a group of children enjoying a birthday party can be found on Chairborough Road in High Wycombe, Buckinghamshire. The pet shop owned by Peter Cushing in one of the best episodes, "The Silent Scream," can be found at 68 Broad Street in Chesham, Buckinghamshire.

Afterword: Location Hunting
by Simon Flynn

It's been quite some time now since Derek Pykett asked me to take some photographs of a few locations in the south of England.

At first I received a short list of about ten, which turned out to be the first of many, and after about four lists and over 50 locations later I'm here. But what took place in between was a highly enjoyable and rewarding journey.

I initially offered to help for many reasons. Firstly, I'm one of life's helpful people (a dwindling breed now). Secondly, it would be rewarding working on a book and having my name and photographs in print. Thirdly, I know, admire, and like Derek Pykett, a truly gracious person and gentleman of the old school, another dwindling breed! Lastly, I find the subject interesting and I think it's a great idea for a book.

Since doing it, I have put in a huge effort, many hours of driving, writing — not to mention the expense of photograph development! Why have I done it? Not for money or recognition, but because I loved every minute of it.

The more places I visited, the more the bug got hold of me, and I'd be phoning Derek inquiring about other addresses and suggesting film titles.

I have been stopped by security guards, barked at by vicious guard dogs, been caught on barbed wire, stung by nettles, climbed hills, been asked to leave (at least three times), and even got called back into a company head office to leave my details. But I've had a laugh, and sometimes felt like the paparazzi working for the *Daily Express*. Not resting until I got Derek a good photograph!

However, I wouldn't have changed a thing. It has been of great interest to me to see where the locations of many interesting and important British horror films were made.

Among the most memorable to me were New Lodge in Windsor, which was just like going onto the set of *Asylum* (1972). The building is totally unchanged and the film is a firm favorite of mine.

Rotherfield House in Hampshire from *House of the Long Shadows* (1982) is a fine house. And of course *Long Shadows* is a memorable and important film: the end of an era. It is Pete Walker's last film and one of the last nostalgic horror films of its kind, featuring Cushing, Lee, Price, Carradine and Keith. None of the five would go on to make many horror films after that.

Oakley Court was of course an important building to visit, as it was probably used in more horror films than any other house. It is a most stunningly beautiful building on fabulous grounds.

Thorpe House in Surrey from *The Creeping Flesh* was also of great importance, because it had eluded Derek for so long. It was on his must-have hit list.

Another place of real interest to me was the Dashwood Mausoleum from *To the Devil a Daughter*, as it is such a powerful building in such a peaceful area.

But of all, Wykehurst Place (Hell House) made everything else look tame. Totally unique and terrifying.

This process has been a journey I have enjoyed very much and I feel privileged and honored to have helped Derek and to have visited these wonderfully interesting places.

Haywards Heath, West Sussex

Bibliography

Bard, Robert. *Elstree & Borehamwood Past*. London: Historical Publications Ltd, 2006.
Barnes, Alan & Marcus Hearn. *The Hammer Story*. United Kingdom: Titan Books Ltd, 1998.
Bryce, Allan. *Amicus: The Studio that Dripped Blood*. United Kingdom: Stray Cat, 2000.
Del Vecchio, Deborah, and Tom Johnson. *Peter Cushing: The Gentle Man of Horror and His 91 Films*. Jefferson, NC: McFarland, 1993.
Elliot, John. *Elliot's Guide to Films on Video*. United Kingdom: Boxtree, 1990.
Gifford, Denis. *A Pictorial History of Horror Films*. London: Hamlyn, 1973.
Halliwell, Leslie. *Halliwell's Film & Video Guide*. United Kingdom: HarperCollins, 1977.
Jones, Stephen. *The Illustrated Frankenstein Movie Guide*. United Kingdom: Titan Books Ltd, 1994.
Kinsey, Wayne. *Hammer Films: The Bray Studio Years*. London: Reynolds & Hearn Ltd, 2002.
Miller, David. *The Peter Cushing Companion*. London: Reynolds & Hearn Ltd, 2000.
Reeves, Tony. *The Worldwide Guide to Movie Locations*. United Kingdom: Titan Books Ltd, 2003.
Rigby, Jonathan. *Christopher Lee: The Authorised Screen History*. London: Reynolds & Hearn Ltd, 2001.
Threadgall, Derek. *Shepperton Studios: An Independent View*. London: BFI Publishing, 1994.
Topping, Keith. *A Vault of Horror: A Book of So Great (and Not So Great) British Horror Movies from 1956–1974*. United Kingdom: Telos Publishing Ltd, 2004.
Warren, Patricia. *British Film Studios*. London: B.T. Batsford Ltd, 1995.

Index

Films listed in ***bold italics*** appear as main entries in the text.

The Abominable Doctor Phibes (1971) 11, 43, 188
Ackland, Joss 72
Adam, Robert 148, 155, 170
The Adventures of Robin Hood (television series) 143
Agutter, Jenny 12
Aldenham 147–148
Alice in Wonderland (1903) 142
Allen, Patrick 91
Alnwick Castle 148–149
An American Werewolf in London (1981) 12–14, 146, 189
Amicus Films 5, 39, 112, 145, 162
And Now the Screaming Starts (1972) 14–15, 168, 187
Annen, Glory 100
The Anniversary (1968) 15–16, 188
Anson, Admiral Lord 166
Anulka 124
Armathwaite Hall Hotel 79
Armstrong, Hugh 36
Ashfield, Kate 105
Ashurst, Sir William 161
Assante, Armand 77
Asylum (1972) 16–17, 45, 167, 187, 196
The Asylum (2000) 17–18, 189
Attenborough, Lord 115, 140, 155, 181
Aubyn, Colonel John St. 173
The Avengers (television series) 11, 140, 176
Avery, Sir William 168
The Awakening (1980) 18, 89, 188

Badham, John 151, 173
Baker, Tom 89, 125
Balcon, Michael 138
Ball, Nicholas 191
Bancroft, Anne 49
Bannen, Ian 40, 128, 157

Barber, Glynis 45
Barker, Will 138
Barnes Hospital 84
Barrie, J.M. 146
Barry, Sir Charles 183
Barry, Edward Middleton 183
Barry Lyndon (1975) 164
Bartholomew, Richard 177
Bates, Ralph 50, 73, 114
Batman (1989) 164
Bayldon, Geoffrey 17
Beacham, Stephanie 14, 43, 75, 93, 168
The Beast in the Cellar (1970) 19, 189
The Beast Must Die (1973) 20, 189
The Beatles 49, 146, 154
Beaton, Norman 191
Becket (1964) 149
Bennett, Hywel 49
Betjeman, Sir John 181
Bhaktivedanta Manor 49, 148
Birch, Thora 67
Bird, Norman 191
The Black Cat (1981) 21–22, 187
Black Memory (1947) 136
Black Park 24, 44, 53, 82, 100, 114, 122
The Black Torment (1964) 22, 178, 188
Blackmail (1929) 139
Blade Runner (1982) 146
Blenheim Palace 55, 81, 149–150
Bless 'Em All (1949) 136
Blind Terror (1971) 22–23, 187
Blood Beast Terror (1968) 9, 23, 158, 188
Blood on Satan's Claw (1970) 23–24, 189
Blue Murder at St. Trinians (1957) 145
Bluebell Railway 19
Boehm, Carl 98
Boot, Sir Charles 143
Boulton, David 157
Bradley, Doug 66

200 Index

Brando, Marlon 93
Bray Studios 40, 88, 101, 135–136
Briant, Shane 162
Bricket Wood Station 92
Brides of Dracula (1960) 9, 24, 168, 187
Brighton's West Pier 51
British Film Institute 5
Brocket Hall 92, 96, 150–151
Brosnan, Pierce 191
Brown, Capability 166
Browne, Pamela 91
Bruce, Brenda 98
Brynner, Yule 16, 40
Bulwer-Lytton, Edward 163
Bulwer-Lytton, Elizabeth 163
Burton, Richard 140, 149
Burton, Tim 164, 176
Bushey Film Studios 26, 136–137
Bygraves, Max 136
Byrne, Gabriel 61
Byron, Lord 151
Bysshop, Thomas 171

Caine, Michael 77, 79, 171, 176
Caldecote Towers 11
Camelot Castle 5, 42, 151–152
Carradine, John 9, 196
Carreras, Enrique 135
Carreras, James 135, 136
Carreras, Michael 135
Carrington (1995) 155
Carry On — Don't Lose Your Head (1966) 155
Carry On Screaming (1966) 25–26, 187
Carson, John 191
Carter, Michael 13
Castle Acre Priory 119, 152
Castle Sinister (1932) 5, 26, 136, 188
Chambers, Sir William 175
Chaney, Lon, Jr. 9, 130, 168
Chantry 16
Chaplin (1992) 155, 181
Chaplin, Charlie 154
Charles, Prince 174
Child, Sir Francis 170, 171
Children of the Damned (1964) 26, 188
Chislehurst Caves 75, 153–154
Churchill, Lady Clementine 150
Churchill, John 149
Churchill, Sir Winston 55, 150, 154, 174
Chute, Sir Charles 178
Chute, John 178
Chute, William Wiggett 178
Cilento, Diane 129
Clay, Nicholas 168
Cleese, John 156
Clegg, Tom 191
Cliveden House Hotel 55, 154–155
A Clockwork Orange (1971) 27, 140, 188
Coen, Guido 146
Colditz (television series) 139
Cole, George 123

Collins, Joan 50, 73
Collins, Lewis 77
The Comeback (1977) 27–29, 189
Connery, Sean 140
The Constant Husband (1955) 145
Cooper, Gary 140
Cope, Kenneth 91
Corman, Roger 120, 152
Costner, Kevin 149
Count Dracula (1977) 29–30, 180, 189
Cox, Brian 191
Craig, Michael 125
Craig, Wendy 90
Crawford, Joan 120, 167
Craze (1974) 30, 177, 189
Creep (2004) 30, 188
The Creeping Flesh (1972) 6, 31, 177, 189, 196
Cribbins, Bernard 56
Cromwell, Oliver 175
Crucible of Terror (1971) 32, 187
The Cruel Sea (1953) 138
Cruise, Tom 156, 181
Cry of the Banshee (1970) 9, 33, 158, 188
The Crying Game (1992) 145
Culver, Roland 81
Culzean Castle 129, 155–156
Curry, Tim 102
The Curse of Frankenstein (1957) 33, 136, 168, 187
The Curse of the Crimson Altar (1968) 9, 34, 159, 188
Cushing, Peter 7, 9, 24, 31, 33, 43, 54, 68, 70, 72, 76, 86, 87, 89, 91, 113, 122, 123, 136, 140, 141, 145, 158, 166, 168, 176, 177, 191, 196

Daltrey, Roger 80
The Dam Busters (1954) 140
The Dark Eyes of London (1939) 34–35
The Dashwood Mausoleum 118, 196
Davies, Rachel 191
Davies, Rupert 57, 132
The Da Vinci Code (2005) 179
Davis, Bette 16, 128, 140, 157
The Day of the Jackal (1973) 176
Dead of Night (1945) 35–36, 138, 187
Dean, Basil 138
Death Line (1972) 36, 188
De Gaulle, President 168
Demons of the Mind (1972) 36–37, 184, 189
Denberg, Susan 53
Deneuve, Catherine 102
Depp, Johnny 107, 176
Derick, John Macduff 176
The Descent (2005) 37, 189
The Devil Rides Out (1968) 16, 37–38, 140, 156, 188
Dickens, Charles 179
Die Monster Die! (1965) 38–39, 168, 187
Dietrich, Marlene 139
Diffring, Anton 87

Disney, Walt 157
Dr. Terror's House of Horrors (1965) 39, 188
Doctor Who (television series) 141, 159
Donlevy, Brian 101
Donohoe, Amanda 80
Doomwatch (1972) 39–40, 187
Dors, Diana 191
Downey, Robert, Jr. 155
Downside School and Abbey 67
Dracula (1931) 180
Dracula (1958) 40, 187
Dracula (1973) 40–41, 167, 187
Dracula (1979) 5, 41–42, 151, 152, 173, 187
Dracula A.D. 1972 (1971) 42–43, 147, 188
Dracula Has Risen from the Grave (1968) 44, 187
Dream Demon (1988) 45, 188
Duggan, Tommy 96
Dunleavy, Ivan 144
Dunne, Griffin 12
Duval, Shelley 106
Dwyer, Hilary 132, 170

Ealing Studios 137–139
The Eccentric Dancer (1896) 142
Eccleston, Christopher 122
Eddington, Paul 38
Edge of Sanity (1988) 45–46, 188
Edgwarebury Corus Hotel 16, 38, 156
The Egg-Laying Man (1896) 142
Eisenhower, President 155, 185
The Elephant Man (1980) 46–49, 145, 188
Eliot, George 162
Elliot, Denholm 191
Elliott, Sam 80
Elstree Film Studios 16, 106, 139–141, 142
Endless Night (1971) 49, 159, 188
English Heritage 23
Ettington Park Hotel 65, 128, 157
Evans, Edith 30
Evans, Ellen 168
Ewing, Barbara 191

Farmer, Mimsy 22
Farrow, Mia 23, 105
Fear in the Night (1971) 43, 49–50, 148, 188
Finch, Jon 56, 191
Finney, Albert 146
A Fish Called Wanda (1988) 146
Fitzgerald, Lord Otto 168
Flemyng, Robert 23
The Flesh and Blood Show (1972) 50–51, 189
Flynn, Errol 140
Flynn, Simon 6, 7, 183, 195–196
Ford, Harrison 140
Fortunes of War (television series) 139
Foster, Barry 56
Fountains Abbey 97, 157–158
Fowlds, Derek 53
Francis, Freddie 1, 6, 47, 74, 113, 144, 177
Francis, Jan 152

Francis, Kevin 144
Francis, Pamela 6
Frankenstein (1984) 51–52, 189
Frankenstein and the Monster from Hell (1972) 52, 140, 162, 188
Frankenstein Created Woman (1966) 52–53, 189
Frankenstein Must Be Destroyed (1969) 53–54, 176, 189
Frankenstein: The True Story (1973) 7, 54–55, 149, 155, 187
Franklin, Pamela 81
Fraser, John 110
Frensham Common 53, 68
Frenzy (1972) 55–56, 144, 188
Frightmare (1974) 56–57, 189
From Beyond the Grave (1972) 57–58, 162, 188
Frost, Nick 105
Fulci, Lucio 21
Fulmer Grange 26
Funny Man (1994) 59, 182, 189

Gaddesden Place 61, 80
Galbo, Christine 83
Gandhi (1982) 146
The Gay Divorcee (1934) 2
Geeson, Judy 40, 50, 75, 153
George, Susan 110
The Ghoul (1933) 59, 141, 188
The Ghoul (1974) 59–60, 144, 187
Gibson, Alan 191
Gielgud, John 48
Gilbert, Sir William Schwenck 159
Gleeson, Brendan 121
GoldenEye (1995) 176
Goodall, Frederick 159
Goring, Marius 191
Gothic (1986) 60–61, 188
Gough, Michael 67, 81, 104, 164
Grade, Michael 144
Grant, Angela 112
Grant, Hugh 80
Gray, Charles 38
Great Expectations (1946) 174
The Greed of William Hart (1948) 136
Greene, Richard 113, 143
Gregory, Gregory 159
Gresham, Sir Thomas 170
Grim's Dyke Hotel 9, 23, 33, 34, 49, 64, 158–159

Hadley Common 43
Hagen, Julius 146
Half Light (2006) 61–62, 139, 189
Hambleden 21, 107
Hammer Films 5, 9, 33, 63, 90, 114, 135, 136, 140, 142, 162, 175, 191
Hammer House of Horror (television series) 191–194
Hampden House 191, 194

202   Index

Hands of the Ripper (1971) 63, 175, 188
A Hard Day's Night (1964) 146
Hardy, Robert 37
Harlaxton Manor 66, 159–160
Harris, Julie 65
Harris, Naome 121
Harris, Richard 140
Harrison, George 49
Harry Potter 107, 149
Harvey, Sir Robert 152
The Hasty Heart (1949) 139
Haunted (1995) 64, 172, 189
Haunted House of Horror (1969) 64, 159, 188
The Haunting (1963) 64–65, 142, 157, 189
The Haunting (1999) 65–66, 160, 188
Hawkins, Jack 116
Heatherden Hall 60, 143, 144
The Hellfire Club (1960) 166
Hellraiser (1987) 66, 188
Hendrix, Jimi 154
Hendry, Ian 116
Hepburn, Audrey 16, 140
Hepworth, Cecil 142
Herkomer, Sir Hubert Von 136, 137
Hermit's Chapel 96, 160–161
Hermon, Edward 182
Heston, Charlton 18
Highgate Cemetery 52, 58, 112, 161–162
Hill, James 171
Hinds, Anthony 135
Hinds, William 135
Hinton, Sean 139
Hitchcock, Alfred 139, 140, 144
Hoffman, Dustin 110
The Hole (2001) 5, 66–67, 136, 187
Holland, Brian 5, 7
Hopkins, Anthony 47
Hordern, Michael 116
Horror Hospital (1973) 67, 164, 188
The Hound of the Baskervilles (1959) 67–68, 189
The House in Nightmare Park (1972) 68–69, 168, 187
House of Mortal Sin (1975) 69, 189
The House of Temperley (1913) 146
House of the Long Shadows (1982) 9, 69–70, 188, 196
House of Whipcord (1974) 2, 70–71, 165, 188
The House That Dripped Blood (1970) 71–72, 145, 189
Houston, Donald 110
Howell, Peter 182
Howerd, Frankie 69, 168
The Hunger (1983) 72–73, 188
Hunnicutt, Gayle 81
Hunton Park 85
Hurt, John 48
Hussein, Saddam 165
Huth, Henry 184

I Don't Want to Be Born (1975) 73, 188
An Ideal Husband (1947) 145
An Ideal Husband (1999) 139
The Importance of Being Earnest (2002) 139
Indiana Jones 140
The Innocents (1961) 73–74, 153, 189
Inseminoid (1980) 74–75, 188
Interview with the Vampire (1994) 5, 75, 181, 188
Irving, Henry 179
Irving, Penny 71, 165
Island of Terror (1966) 75–76, 187

Jack the Ripper (1988) 5, 76–78, 171, 176, 188
James, Sidney 136, 155
Jane Eyre (television) 140
Jekyll, Gertrude 164
Jekyll & Hyde (1990) 5, 78–79, 176, 188
Jones, Andy 165
Jones, Barry 110
Jones, Freddie 54, 103
Jordan, Louis 149, 180
Jupp, Dr. Ralph 146
Jurgens, Curt 125

Karlin, Miriam 27
Karloff, Boris 9, 34, 39, 59, 141, 159, 168
Keith, Sheila 29, 57, 69, 71, 196
Kellerman, Barbara 191
Kennedy, Sir Thomas 155
Kensel Green Cemetery 116
Kentwell Hall 133, 162–163
Kerr, Deborah 74
Killer's Moon (1978) 79, 187
Kimberly, Maggie 133
Kind Hearts and Coronets (1949) 138
A Kind of Loving (1962) 145
King Charles Street 77
Kings Rhapsody (1955) 140
Kinnear, Roy 114
Kinski, Nastassia 119
Knebworth House 67, 80, 87, 163–164
Korda, Alexander 145
The Krays (1990) 181
Kubrick, Stanley 140, 142, 156, 164

Ladd, Cheryl 79
The Ladykillers (1955) 138
The Lair of the White Worm (1988) 79–80, 164, 188
Lamb, Lady Caroline 151
Lamb, Sir Mathew 151
Lamont, Duncan 53
Landis, John 13, 146
Langella, Frank 5, 42, 151
Last of the Summer Wine (television series) 140
Laughton, Charles 139
Laurenson, James 164
The Lavender Hill Mob (1951) 138
Lavenham 133, 164

Index   203

Lawrence of Arabia (1962) 174
Lawson, Leigh 191
Lawson, Sarah 91
Lean, David 144, 174
Leaver, Don 191
Leavesden Film Studios 107
Led Zeppelin 163
Lee, Christopher 9, 33, 34, 43, 44, 59, 70, 89, 91, 103, 114, 119, 129, 136, 140, 156, 159, 162, 182, 196
The Legacy (1978) 80, 166, 189
The Legend of Hell House (1973) 15, 80–82, 149, 183, 185, 189
Legend of the Werewolf (1974) 82, 144, 187
Leigh, Vivien 139
Leoni, Giacomo 166
Lester, Richard 146
Letchmore Heath 127, 147, 148
Leybourne, George 181
Life with the Lyons (1954) 135
Lime Grove Studios 59, 141
Littledean Jail 71, 165
Littleton Park House 17, 20, 100, 144
Liverpool Street Station 48
The Living Dead at the Manchester Morgue (1974) 5, 82–84, 188
Lochinch Castle 129
Lockwood, Margaret 141
Long Time Dead (2002) 84, 188
Look Back in Anger (1959) 140
Loren, Sophia 16
Loseley Park House 80, 165–166
Loudon, Norman 144, 145
Lovelock, Ray 83
The L-Shaped Room (1962) 145
Lucan, Arthur 142
Lucas, George 140
Lugosi, Bela 9, 35, 88, 90, 142, 180
Lust for a Vampire (1970) 84–85, 188
Lutyens, Edwin 163
Lynch, David 49
Lytton, Sir Robert 163

MacCorkindale, Simon 191
MacGinnis, Niall 92, 151
Macmillan, Harold 154
Macnee, Patrick 140
Madhouse (1973) 85–86, 189
The Madness of King George (1994) 174
Malleson, Miles 98
The Man in Black (1950) 135
Mappin, John 152
Markham, David 113
Marx, Karl 162
Masks and Faces (1917) 146
The Masks of Death (1984) 86–87, 187
Mason, James 141
The Masque of the Red Death (1964) 120
Massey, Daniel 125
McDowall, Roddy 81
McDowell, Malcolm 27

McEnery, Peter 191
McShane, Kitty 142
Medwin, Michael 136
Megahy, Francis 191
Merrow, Jane 91, 175
MGM Film Studios 141–142
Michelle, Ann 127
Michelle, Vicki 127
Milland, Ray 168
Mills, Hayley 49
Mills, John 87, 124
Minnelli, Liza 181
Mitchell, Norman 52, 162
Mitchell, Oswald 136
Moby Dick (1956) 140
The Monster Club (1980) 43, 87, 164, 188
Monty Python's Flying Circus (television series) 139
Moor Park Mansion 123, 166
Moore, Demi 62
Moore, Roger 140
Morden, Lt. Col. Grant 143
More, Sir William 165
Morell, Andre 68
Morris, Marianne 124
Morris, Robert 53
Morris, William 176
Mother Riley Meets the Vampire (1952) 9, 87–88, 142, 189
Mower, Patrick 33, 156
The Mummy (1959) 88–89, 187
The Mummy Returns (2001) 89, 188
Munro, Caroline 11, 43
Murder on the Orient Express (1974) 140
Murphy, Cillian 121
Murray, Barbara 113
The Mutations (1974) 89, 168, 187
The Mystery of the Mary Celeste (1935) 9, 89–90, 142, 189

Nail, Jimmy 45
The Naked Edge (1961) 140
The Nanny (1965) 90, 140, 188
National Trust 37, 62, 155, 156, 171, 173, 178
Naughton, David 12
Neal, Patricia 91
Neame, Christopher 43
Neeson, Liam 160
Neill, Sam 96, 151, 158
Nelson, Admiral 174
Nettlefold Studios 9, 88, 142–143
Never Say Never Again (1983) 140
Neville, John 110
New Lodge 17, 120, 167, 195
Newton, Robert 139
Nicholas, Paul 23
Nicholson, Jack 106
The Night Digger (1971) 91, 168, 187
Night of the Big Heat (1967) 91, 187
Night of the Demon (1957) 92, 151, 188
The Nightcomers (1971) 92–93, 187

Nightingale, Florence 174
Nineteen Eighty Four (television) 141
Nothing but the Night (1972) 93–94, 176, 189
Notting Hill (1999) 139

Oakley Court 9, 14, 24, 33, 39, 41, 69, 89, 91, 94, 102, 124, 130, 167–168, 196
O'Brien, Richard 102, 168
Ogilvy, Ian 14, 108, 133, 170
O'Hara, Maureen 139
The Old Dark House (1962) 94, 168, 187
Old Netherne Hospital 18
The Old Wood Carver (1913) 136
Oliver Twist (1948) 144
Olivier, Ernest 168
Olivier, Laurence 5, 42, 139, 152, 179, 181
The Omen (1976) 94–95, 189
Omen III — The Final Conflict (1981) 95–97, 151, 158, 160, 189
Orford Castle 133, 169–170
Osterley Park House 77, 110, 170–171
O'Toole, Peter 149
Owen, Bill 29

Padbury, Wendy 23
Palance, Jack 30, 41, 167, 177
Palmer, Sir Thomas 171
Parham House 64, 171–172
Patrick, Nigel 113
PC 49 (1951) 135
Pearce, Terry 7, 112
Pearson, Clive 171
Peck, Gregory 16, 95, 140
Peckinpah, Sam 146
Peel, David 24, 168
Peeping Tom (1960) 97–98, 188
Pegg, Simon 105
Perkins, Anthony 45
Persecution (1974) 98–99, 187
Phantom of the Opera (1962) 99, 188
Phillips, Judith 162
Phillips, Patrick 162
Phillips, Robin 113
Phipps, John Lewis 168
Piccadilly Circus 13
Pinewood Studios 37, 60, 75, 143–144, 145, 175
Pink Floyd 154, 163
Pitt, Brad 181
Pitt, Ingrid 123
Plague of the Zombies (1965) 99–100, 187
Pleasence, Donald 42, 89, 152, 168
Polperro 40
Porter, Eric 175
Porth Dinllaen 62
Potente, Franka 30
Potter, Ruth 7
Potts, Andrew Thirlwall 5
Powell, Michael 144
Powell, Robert 17, 52, 167

Prey (1977) 100, 189
Price, Dennis 116
Price, Vincent 9, 11, 33, 70, 86, 116, 119, 133, 152, 158, 163, 164, 170, 196
The Private Life of Sherlock Holmes (1970) 176
Private's Progress (1956) 145
The Professionals (television series) 176
Pyrford Court 95, 113
Pyrford Place 86

Quatermass II (television) 141
Quatermass 2 (1957) 101, 136, 188
The Quatermass Xperiment (1955) 100–101, 136, 179, 187
Queen 163
Quinn, Aidan 64, 172
Quinn, Anthony 16
Quinn, Patricia 102, 191

Randall & Hopkirk — Deceased (television series) 176
Rank, J. Arthur 141, 143
Raven, Mike 32
Raymond, Gary 191
Reagan, Ronald 16, 139
The Red Shoes (1948) 144
Redgrave, Jemma 45
Reed, Carol 144
Rees, Angharad 175
Reeves, Michael 164, 170
Remick, Lee 95
Repulsion (1965) 101–102, 188
Revill, Clive 81
Rhodes, Matthew John 176
Richardson, Natasha 61
Richardson, Sir Ralph 162
Ripley Castle 52
Ripper, Michael 24
Roberts, Rachel 146
Robertson, Peter Forbes 76
Robin Hood: Prince of Thieves (1991) 149
Robinson, Andrew 66
Robinson, Bernard 40
The Rocky Horror Picture Show (1975) 102, 168, 187
The Rolling Stones 163
Room at the Top (1958) 145
Roosevelt, President 154
Rosenberg, Max J. 145
Ross, Katherine 80
Rotherfield House 9, 70, 196
Royal Mint 48
The Ruling Class (1972) 2
Rundle, Letty 152
Russell, Ken 164
Ryan, Sally-Anne 7

The Saint (television series) 140
St. Agnes 32
St. Dunstan's Church 26

Index 205

St. James Church 23
St. Mary the Virgin 36
St. Michael's & All Angels Church 83
St. Michael's Mount 42, 172–173
St. Paul's Cathedral 63, 173–175
Salvin, Anthony 159
Sanders, George 127
Sands, Julian 61
Sarandon, Susan 73
Sasdy, Peter 191
The Satanic Rites of Dracula (1972) 102–103, 188
Satan's Slave (1976) 103–104, 189
Saturday Night, Sunday Morning (1960) 146
Sawston Hall 93
Say, Sir Richard Hall 168
Scott, Major 177
Scott, Ridley 145
Scott, Tony 145
Scott of the Antarctic (1948) 138
Scratchwood Nature Reserve 114
Secret Ceremony (1968) 104–105, 188
Sellers, Peter 156, 181
Seymour, Edward 175
Sharp, Anthony 69
Sharp, Don 191
Shaun of the Dead (2004) 5, 105, 139, 188
Shaw, George Bernard 146, 154
Shaw, Norman 159
Shelley, Mary Wollstonecraft 7
Shepperton Studios 39, 58, 143, 144–145
The Shining (1980) 105–106, 140, 188
Shirley, Evelyn Philip 157
Shirley, John 157
The Singing Detective (television series) 139
Skeggs, Roy 191
Slaughter, Todd 136
Sleepy Hollow (1999) 106–107, 176, 187
Somerset House 77, 79, 107, 175–176
Son of Dracula (1974) 107–108, 189
The Sorcerers (1967) 108, 188
Spall, Timothy 45
Spencer, Lady Diana 174
Spielberg, Steven 140
Stage Fright (1950) 139
Standing, John 80
Stanmore Hall 54, 94, 176
Star Wars (1976) 140, 141
Star Wars—Episode II (2002) 139
Starr, Ringo 108
Stephens, Harvey 95
Stoker, Bram 7, 9, 30, 149, 159, 173, 180
Stourton, Ted 152
Straw Dogs (1971) 108–110, 146, 187
A Study in Terror (1965) 110, 171, 189
Styles, Benjamin Hoskins 166
Subotsky, Milton 145
Superman II (1981) 146
Svengali (1954) 142
The Swan Inn 91
Sweeney, George 77

Tales from the Crypt (1972) 7, 110–113, 145, 162, 189
Talk of the Devil (1936) 144
Taste the Blood of Dracula (1970) 43, 113–114, 162, 189
Taylor, Elizabeth 16, 105
Taylor, Lili 66, 160
10 Rillington Place (1970) 114–115, 189
Theatre of Blood (1973) 115–117, 189
Theatre of Death (1966) 117–118, 189
Thomas, Terry 125
Thompson, Emma 155
Thornhill, Sir James 166
Thorpe House 6, 31, 177, 196
Thunderbirds (2003) 155
To the Devil a Daughter (1976) 118–119, 187, 196
Todd, Richard 140
The Tomb of Ligeia (1964) 119–120, 152, 189
Tomorrow Never Dies (1997) 176
Tonson, Jacob 135
Tower Bridge 35, 56
Townsend, Isaac 177
Tritton, P.A. 171
Trog (1970) 120, 167, 187
Troughton, Patrick 52, 95, 162
Turner, John 22, 178
Turner, Lana 99
28 Days Later (2002) 121–122, 189
Twickenham Film Studios 13, 145–146
Twins of Evil (1971) 122, 187
2001: A Space Odyssey (1968) 142
Tyburn Productions 144
Tykes Water Lake & Bridge 43

UFO (television series) 142
University College 18, 89
Urquhart, Robert 191

The Vampire Lovers (1970) 122–123, 166, 188
Vampyres (1974) 123–124, 168, 187
Vanbrugh, Sir J. 149
Van de Weyer, Jean Sylvain 167
Vault of Horror (1973) 124–125, 189
Village of the Damned (1960) 125–127, 147, 148, 188
Villiers, James 90
Virgin Witch (1971) 127, 189
The Vyne 22, 177–178

Walker, Pete 1–3, 196
Wall Hall Mansion 90, 123
Warbeck, David 22
The Watcher in the Woods (1980) 127–128, 187
Waverley Abbey 122, 165
Weinstein, Hannah 143
Welwyn Film Studios 35
West, Fred 165
West Wycombe Village 22
Westminster Abbey 101, 147, 171, 178–179

Where Eagles Dare (1969) 142
Whisky Galore (1948) 138
Whitby 30, 179–180
Whiting, Leonard 55
Whitstable 9
The Who 154
The Wicked Lady (1945) 141
The Wicker Man (1973) 128–129, 156, 189
Wickes, David 5, 171, 176
Wilder, Billy 176
Williams, Kenneth 26
Wilton, John 181
Wilton, Penelope 105
Wilton's Music Hall 75, 180–181
Witchcraft (1964) 9, 130, 168, 187
The Witches (1990) 130, 187

Witchfinder General (1968) 130–133, 163, 164, 170, 189
Wolfit, Donald 142
Woodward, Edward 129
Wren, Christopher 173
Wuthering Heights (television) 140
Wyfold Court 59, 181–183
Wykehurst Place 15, 37, 81, 108, 183–186, 196
Wymark, Patrick 23

Young, Robert 191

Zeta-Jones, Catherine 160
Zucchi, Antonio 155
Zulu (1964) 146

www.ingramcontent.com/pod-product-compliance
Ingram Content Group UK Ltd.
Pitfield, Milton Keynes, MK11 3LW, UK
UKHW042000140426
5217IPUK00015B/906